TORAH WISDOM
FOR TURBULENT TIMES

EMUNAH, FAMILY, AND THE FUTURE

RABBI DOVID ABENSON

To view over thirty haskamos from Gedolim, Dayanim, and Mechanchim, as well as recommendations from parents and students, visit my website: shaarhatamud.com

First published 2024

Published by Targum Publishers
Shlomo ben Yosef 131a/1
Jerusalem 9380581
editor@targumpublishers.com

Distributed by Rabbi Dovid Abenson
1 Giti Rd.
Lakewood NJ 08701, USA

Tel/Whatsapp/Text 848-367-1740
ravabenson@shaarhatalmud.com
Website shaarhatalmud.com

An Abenson publication

Printed in Israel

For consultations, remedial support, or speaking engagements at your yeshiva, school, or kehilla, contact Rabbi Dovid Abenson. He also specialises in upgrading and strengthening Kodesh Departments.

May this sefer be a zechus in memory
of my parents and in-laws,
and my uncle and aunt

ר׳ אברהם בן יעקב ז״ל

דבורה בת צבי חנוך ע״ה

ר׳ שאול מרדכי בן יוסף ז״ל

רחל לאה בת חיים ע״ה

ר׳ משה בן יעקב ז״ל

שרה לאה בת דוד ע״ה

CONTENTS

PART ONE: Torah Perspectives on Sensitive Topics

Giving Birth to New Perspectives 13

The Wedding Night 15

Time to Defrost the freezer 24

Maidservants, Mother: Birds and the Importance of Mesorah 26

IN G-D WE TRUST? The Supreme Court's acceptance of Toeva
    Marriages 33

Bris Milah: Identifying the Real Deal 36

PART TWO: Ancient Perspectives on Current Events

Coronavirus Bringing the lesson home 42

Safety Measures to Prevent the Spread of "Dis-affection" 46

Freedom Convoy 2022 52

An Ice Storm Story 56

Conversation with a Pastor 58

The Design of a Shul, and What is it Meant to Teach Us? 62

A Farewell Speech 67

What We Can Learn from the Holocaust? 76

The October 7 Massacre 74

"A Wake-Up Call from Heaven: Understanding the Challenges of Our Times Through Torah"..75

Reflections on Iran's Threats Through the Lens of the Midrash Rabbah (*Esther*) 83

From Haman to Hamas: Reflections on Wealth, Power, and Divine Justice 87

Hashem Will Never Forsake Us...92

The Verdict on President Donald Trump: A Jewish Perspective............97

An Open Miracle by Hashem for the World to see.................................103

The Fifth Galus 108

PART 3

"A Signed Letter from President Donald J. Trump Praising and Blessing Rabbi Dovid Abenson for the Tremendous Work He Does for the Jewish People"...115

Other Books By Rabbi Dovid Abenson 127

OVERVIEW

The book is divided into three parts, offering profound insights into Torah perspectives, addressing sensitive topics, and exploring current events through the lens of the Torah. This comprehensive work combines timeless wisdom with contemporary relevance.

Part One: Torah Perspectives on Sensitive Topics

This section tackles challenging issues, deeply grounded in Torah wisdom. It lays the foundation for the rest of the book by providing a robust framework of Torah values on matters that resonate with many readers.

With the invaluable advice of my revered Rebbe, HaRav Mattisyahu Chaim Salomon זצ"ל, and through Hashgacha Pratis, I have been privileged to rediscover a groundbreaking method that was potentially lost for nearly 1,500 years. This method, rooted in the wisdom of the Gemara, allows parents to influence the gender of their child with remarkable accuracy when applied meticulously according to Torah principles.

Also included in this section are explorations of several sensitive issues, including:

- The sanctity of marriage as a holy union between a man and a Woman.
- Why boys should seek to marry at 18 years of age, as per Halacha, rather than delaying entering shidduchim, as is common today.

- A deep explanation of the challenging topic in Parshas Mishpatim about why a daughter sold into servitude does not go free when other slaves do, and the requirement for the master or his son to marry her.

- The Torah's response to the Supreme Court's legalization of same-gender marriages.

- The distinctions between Muslim circumcision and the Jewish Bris Milah.

As the world's morality crumbles around us, we need the Torah more than ever to provide grounding. Eitz Chaim hi l'machazikim bo—the Torah is a tree of life for those who hold fast to it. My hope is that this material will strengthen readers' emunah in the Torah, improve unity and relationships within marriage, and convey the eternal wisdom of our chachamim, serving as a beacon of truth in these dark times.

Part Two: Current Events in the Light of Torah

This section delves into modern-day events, examining them through the prism of Torah wisdom. It explores how contemporary geopolitical and social issues reflect the prophetic insights of the Torah, demonstrating the ongoing relevance of ancient teachings in today's world.

Part Three: A Signed Letter from President Donald J. Trump: Praising and Blessing Rabbi Dovid Abenson for the Tremendous Work He Does for the Jewish People.

The letter highlights the intersection of political leadership and religious values, providing readers with a unique perspective on how modern leadership impacts the Jewish world. This addition further emphasises the relevance of Torah values in shaping our understanding of current events and global leadership.

Rabbi Dovid Abenson

PART ONE:
TORAH PERSPECTIVES ON SENSITIVE TOPICS

GIVING BIRTH TO NEW
PERSPECTIVES

My learning with a retired gynecologist opened up new perspectives on a difficult Gemara for me, and a deepened appreciation for the wisdom of Chazal for him.

The story begins several years ago when a Baal Teshuva (BT) from Detroit returned from studying in Eretz Yisroel but continued to face learning challenges. He approached his Rabbi in Detroit for help. His Rabbi mentioned that he had previously spoken to Rav Mattisyahu about returning BTs who were facing similar dilemmas. Rav Mattisyahu had recommended Rabbi Dovid Abenson, who had been very successful in teaching BTs.

After several close sessions, my talmid asked if I could reach out to his father to help him improve his Hebrew reading skills and hopefully reconnect with his heritage. It turned out that his father had had challenging relationships with rabbis in the past, feeling intimidated and sometimes belittled. This discomfort with the religious community began as early as his bar mitzvah when a rabbi scolded him for not wearing the right clothing. This incident left a lasting negative impression and resulted in difficulties with Hebrew reading.

The father was a retired gynecologist, a man who delivered over 10,000 babies in his over four decades' long career. He is knowledgable and intelligent and began to connect well to our learning. One particularly encouraging moment, as the son shared with me, was when the doctor had asked me a question, and received a thoughtful response. He felt a sense of accomplishment – the joy of 'stumping the rabbi.' It was a stark departure from the feelings of inadequacy he had experienced in the past.

I was moved to hear that, through our learning, this gentleman, who was once completely secular, has not only embraced Judaism but has developed a love for learning. From struggling with Hebrew to now being able to read it, his journey is a testament to the transformative power of personalised and respectful Torah education.

I also gained tremendously from this relationship.

His background in his medical specialty led us on some fascinating journeys through chumash and the meforshim particularly where the discussions revolve around birth and conception. At first glance we found Rashis and Chazals that seemed to contradict the science as learned and practiced by the doctor, but a deeper investigation through the meforshim revealed a more nuanced understanding. It was a fascinating journey of discovery for both of us. My talmid gained an increasing respect for Torah wisdom.

He was particularly amazed that the Gemara (*Niddah* 31a) describes how the manner of conception determines the sex of the fetus conceived. It coincided completely with a successful method he had explained over the years to many couples who were trying to conceive a boy after many girls (or vice versa). He was able to completely understand chazals that had stumped my own Torah scholar acquaintances!

When Lot's daughters ran away from Sodom and hid in the cave (*Bereishis* 19:31), the pesukim state:

ותאמר הבכירה אל־הצעירה אבינו זקן ואיש אין בארץ לבוא עלינו כדרך כל־הארץ לכה נשקה את־אבינו יין ונשכבה עמו ונחיה מאבינו זרע

And the elder said to the younger, "Our father is old, and there is no man on earth to come to us, as is the custom of all the earth". The text continues: "Come, let us give our father wine to drink, and let us lie with him, and let us bring to life seed from our father."

12

Rashi brings down the *Bereishis Rabbah* (51:8).

איש אין בארץ: סבורות היו שכל העולם נחרב כמו בדור המבול (בראשית רבה)

They thought that the entire world had been destroyed, as in the generation of the flood.

ותהרין שתי בנות־לוט מאביהן

And Lot's two daughters conceived from their father. (Bereishis 19:36)

Rashi again brings down again the *Midrash Rabbah* (51:9)

אף על פי שאין האשה מתעברת מביאה ראשונה, אלו שלטו בעצמן והוציאו ערותן
לחוץ ונתעברו מביאה ראשונה

Although a woman does not conceive from the first intercourse, they controlled themselves and took out their maidenhoods and conceived from the first intercourse.

The gynecologist shared a different viewpoint. Whilst Rashi's explanation is generally accurate, he asserted that, based on his career, there is indeed a minority of individuals who can conceive.

I didn't want to dismiss his insights. So I made a commitment to consult with a talmid chacham with whom I have a kesher, and get back to him.

The talmid chacham told me that in Parshas Lech L'cha, when Abraham married Hagar *(Bereishis* 16:4), Rashi said she got pregnant from the first intimacy. Rashi quotes *Bereishis Rabbah* (4:45):

ויבא אל הגר ותהר (בראשית טז, ד), רבי לוי בר חיתא אמר מביאה ראשונה
נתעברה, אמר רבי אלעזר לעולם אין האשה מתעברת מביאה ראשונה, והכתיב
(בראשית יט, לו): ותהרין שתי בנות לוט מאביהן, אמר רבי תנחומא שלטו בעצמן
והוציאו ערותן ונתעברו כמביאה שניה

"And he went into Hagar, and she conceived" (Bereishis 16:4). Rabbi Levi bar Hayta said: She became pregnant at the first intimacy. Said Rabbi Eleazar: A woman never conceives from the first intimacy. An objection is raised: surely it is written, "So both of Lot's daughters got pregnant by their father" (Bereshis. 19:36)? Said R. Tanhuma. "By an effort of will power they brought forth their virginity and conceived as if it was like a second act of intercourse."

13

So it seemed that Rabbi Levi bar Hayta took the position of the doctor. But this still leaves a question on Rabbi Eleazar, who states clearly that, "A woman cannot conceive by the first intimacy."

The talmid chacham showed me two teshuvas of the Nodah Beyehudah written over two hundred years ago discussing this same question. *(Even HaEzer* 31:3,1 *Even HaEzer* 22:2)

The Nodah Beyehudah concludes that the majority of women cannot get pregnant the first time but there is a minority which can, and that is what Rabbi Eleazar meant עׁׁ״פ רוב (although the majority). This coincided exactly with what the gynecologist had thought from the scientific perspective. The doctor was very impressed.

But we had a further question. Lot's daughters had boys, not girls. The famous gemara in *Niddah* 31a states:

אמר רבי יצחק אמר רבי אמי אשה מזרעת תחילה יולדת זכר איש מזריע תחילה
יולדת נקבה שנאמר אשה כי תזריע וילדה זכר (ויקרא יג, כט).

Rabbi Yitzḥak in the name of Rabbi Ami says: The sex of a fetus is determined at the moment of conception. If the woman emits seed first, she gives birth to a male, and if the man emits seed first, she gives birth to a female, as it is stated: "If a woman bears seed and gives birth to a male" (Vayikra 12:2).

The Sages taught: At first, people would say that if the woman emits seed first she gives birth to a male, and if the man emits seed first, she gives birth to a female. But the Sages did not explain from which verse this matter is derived, until Rabbi Tzadok came and explained that it is derived from the following verse: "These are the sons of Leah, whom she bore to Jacob in Paddan Aram, with his daughter Dinah" (Bereshis 46:15). From the fact that the verse attributes the males to the females, as the males are called: The sons of Leah, and it attributes the females to the males, in that Dinah is called: His daughter, it is derived that if the woman emits seed first she gives birth to a male, whereas if the man emits seed first, she bears a female.

The talmid chacham told me we do not know what that means today.

When I shared the Gemara with the gynecologist, however, it resonated immediately. "It makes perfect sense," he said. Eager to understand his perspective, I inquired, "What do you mean?"

He elaborated as follows:

The Gynaecologist's Tried and Trusted Method of Influencing the Gender of a Child Being Conceived.

Trying for a Boy:

Based on the fact that male sperm swim faster than female sperm, one can time intercourse to enhance one's chances of having a male child. One must defer intercourse till after the woman has ovulated, therefore the egg is waiting for the sperm to arrive, and the initial wave of sperm will be overwhelmingly male.

To do this, I recommend using an ovulation detection kit (approximately $25.00) and testing one's first morning urine beginning around day #12 of the cycle as instructed. As soon as it becomes positive, it means that the LH surge has occurred, and that ovulation should follow in approximately 12 hours. I recommend waiting a full 24 hours to ensure that ovulation has indeed occurred. Have intercourse and the majority of the sperm that will first encounter the egg will be male. If conception occurs, the chances are much increased that it will be a boy.

Trying for a Girl:

Conversely, if trying to have a female infant, one can also try to time intercourse however this is much more difficult. The woman must have very regular cycles. For instance, if she has a 28-day cycle, then one can assume that she is ovulating on day #14. One can have intercourse up to day #12, then stop[*]. The male sperm that arrives first will die. The female sperm which arrives slower will be available when the egg ovulates on day #14. If conception occurs, the chances of a girl would be much increased. Good Luck but remember there are no guarantees.

---

[*] Due to niddah concerns this method may have to be adapted for frum couples

This information is what the Gynecologist had put together from his own medical knowledge, research and experience with patients in over four decades of practice. He shared it with parents trying for a third child where they already had two of the same gender with extremely high success rates. He was literally blown away to see his theories understood and written by Chazal 1500 years ago.

Simultaneously the retired doctor felt closer to Torah and his heritage, seeing its wisdom completely resonating with all he knew from his scientific background and experience with helping couples with their fertility and I was elated to have been enlightened in this difficult piece of Torah that now made so much sense thanks to the doctor's explanations.

My hope is that by publicizing this information many more couples can be helped and we can see the perfect harmony of Hashem's Torah and the world he created therewith.

As Rabbi Ḥanina says (*Ta'anis 7a*):

דאמר רבי חנינא: הרבה למדתי מרבותי ומחבירי יותר מרבותי, ומתלמידי יותר מכולן

"I have learned much from my teachers and even more from my friends, but from my students, I have learned more than from all of them"

THE WEDDING NIGHT

The last sixty years have seen a rapid decline in the area of morality, even to the extent that so-called "orthodox" rabbis advocate for tolerance and acceptance of LGBT communities. In past articles I have shown how the decree against the generation of the flood was sealed once same-sex marriages were legalised. In our generation too, there appears to be a link between governments legalizing and promoting such unions and the apocalyptic events of recent months. The liberal view is that what people do in the privacy of their own homes is their own business, but as we know the Torah perspective is quite the opposite.

The Jewish people are meant to serve Hashem with simcha:

עבדו את־ה׳ בשמחה באו לפניו ברננה

"Serve Hashem with happiness; come before His presence with singing" (Tehillim 100:2).

Additionally we find in:

תחת אשר לא־עבדת את־ה׳ אלקיך בשמחה ובטוב לבב מרב כל

"Because you did not serve Hashem, your God, with happiness and with gladness of heart, when [you had an] abundance of everything" (Devarim 28:47).

The Gemara *(Yevamos 63b)* says the ultimate happiness a person can experience in this world is dependent upon marriage.

אמר רבי תנחום א״ר חנילאי כל אדם שאין לו אשה שרוי בלא שמחה בלא ברכה

בלא טובה בלא שמחה דכתיב (דברים יד, כו) ושמחת אתה וביתך בלא ברכה
דכתיב (יחזקאל מד, ל) להניח ברכה אל ביתך בלא טובה דכתיב (בראשית ב, יח)
לא טוב היות האדם לבדו

*Rabbi Tanḥum said that Rabbi Ḥanilai said: Any man who does
not have a wife is left without happiness without blessing, without
goodness. He proceeds to quote biblical verses to support each part
of his statement. Furthermore the* מהרש"א *says that although Klal
Yisroel is currently in exile, bereft of true joy, the celebration of a new
home is an exception.*

According to the Rambam *(Avel* chapter 14*)*, it's a rabbinical commandment to make the חתן וכלה happy. This is achieved by increasing
simcha at the wedding celebration and by adding a new face at each
שבעה ברוכות *(Kesuvos* 8a). The sixth blessing of the sheva brachos re-
volves around this theme of bringing joy to the bride and groom.

The Divine Presence does not rest upon anyone unless there is
joy *(Shabbos* 30b). We see this is the case of the Neviim, who did not
prophesy whenever they chose, but would prepare themselves, with
music to attain a deep level of joy, as it is written "And it came to pass
when the minstrel played, that the hand of Hashem came upon him".
The music and rejoicing of the wedding then is what enables חתן וכלה to
create the בית נאמן, the house of faithfulness that the couple will build,
since joy increases faithfulness, the intimate connection with Hashem.
The initial creation of the בית נאמן parallels Hashem's creation of the
world. Just as the original creation was completed in seven days, so we
observe seven days of celebration following a wedding in order to complete this holy creation. Where is the source to observe this seven day
celebration? The Yerushalmi in *Kesuvos* 2b writes that Moshe Rabbeinu established שבעת ימי המשתה (Look at פני משה וקרבן העדה there).

The strength of the connection with Hashem upon the creation of
the bayis neeman surpasses that which can be achieved by the man or
the woman as individuals. Hence the simcha associated with a marriage
is greater than the ordinary simcha with which we must serve Hashem.

To understand this deeper we must go back to the first "marriage",

18

that of Adam and Chava.

The Gemara (*Yevamos* 63a) implies that marriage is essential to a man's essence:

א"ר אלעזר כל אדם שאין לו אשה אינו אדם שנאמר (בראשית ה, ב) זכר ונקבה בראם ויקרא את שמם אדם

Rabbi Elazar said: Any man who does not have a wife is not a man, as it is stated: "Male and female He created them… and called their name Adam" (Bereishis 5:2).

Adam refers to male and female as a unit. However in *Pirkei d'Rabbi Eliezer* 12 we learn:

ר' יהודה אומר על שם אדמה שלוקח ממנה נקרא שמו אדם, ר' יהושע בן קרחא אומר על שם בשר ודם נקרא שמו, ומשבנה לו עזר אש שמו והוא אש

Rabbi Yehudah said: Because of the name Adamah (ground) whence he was taken, his name was called Adam. Rabbi Joshua ben Korchah said: He was called Adam because of his flesh and blood (dām). He said to him: Adam! Adam! And when a help-mate had been built for him, his name was called êsh (fire), and she (was called) êsh (fire).

There appears to be a contradiction between these two sources. How can R' Yehoshua ben Karchah say that both names changed to אש when the Torah explicitly states they were called Adam?

The answer is found in the posuk (*Bereishis* 1:27) זכר ונקבה ברא אתם (Male and female He created them). Rashi says here that He created man with two faces, one side a male and one side of female at the original creation afterward he divided them then he built a helper from him as it states (*Bereishis* 2:22):

ויפל ה' אלקים ׀ תרדמה על־האדם ויישן ויקח אחת מצלעתיו ויסגר בשר תחתנה ויבן ה' אלקים ׀ את־הצלע אשר־לקח מן־האדם לאשה ויבאה אל־האדם

So Hashem Elokim cast a deep sleep upon the man; and, while he slept, He took one of his ribs and closed up the flesh at that spot. And Lord Hashem built the bone which he took from the man for a woman and he brought her to the man. Whilst they were one creature, they were called "Adam". After being separated they were both called "esh".

19

How can two fires live together without consuming everything?

מה עשה הקב״ה נתן שמו יו״ד שמו יו״ד ה״א יק, אמר אם הולכים בדרכי ושומרים מצותי הרי שמי נתון ביניהם ומציל אותם מכל צרה, ואם לאו אני נוטל את שמי מביניהם והם נעשים אש והאש אוכלת אש, שני כי אש היא עד אבדון תאכל ובכל תבואתי תשרש

What did the Holy One, blessed be He, do? He put His name (יק) between their (names), saying: If they go in My ways and keep all My precepts, behold My name is given to them, it will deliver them from all distress. If they do not (walk in My ways), behold I will take away My name from their (names), and they will become êsh (fire). And fire consumes fire, as it is said, "For it is a fire that consumeth unto Destruction" (Iyov 31:12). (Pirkei d'rabbi Eliezer 12)

True שמחה can be achieved only when one gets married. A man (איש) and a woman (אשה) together provide a vessel to contain Hashem (יק). By following in His ways, a couple can live together peacefully. If they neglect to maintain the presence of yud and hey, they both become אש, a fire that will consume both of them.

The mitzvah to be fruitful and multiply was given to Adam and is incumbent on every human, Jew and non-Jew alike. So too the seven noahide laws, which include the prohibition of all deviant relationships, apply to all humanity, as the Rambam writes

הלכות מלכים פ״ט ה״ה ״על כן יעזב איש את אביו״ זו אשת אביו. (בראשית ב, כד) ״ואת אמו״ כמשמעה. (בראשית ב, כד) ״ודבק באשתו״ ולא באשת חברו. באשתו ולא בזכור. (בראשית ב, כד) ״והיו לבשר אחד״ להוציא בהמה חיה ועוף שאין הוא והם בשר אחד״

"And so a man will leave his father" (Bereishis 2:24), we learn of the prohibition with his father's wife; "and his mother" (ibid.) – this is learned in its literal sense; from "and cleave to his wife" (ibid.) we deduce – and not his friend's wife; from "his wife or, his woman" (ibid.) – and not with a male. (Homosexuality is explicitly forbidden, and the punishment is סקילה, stoning, Vayikra 18:22.)

Marriage needs to be preserved as a holy union, with Hashem in the centre. This is the cornerstone of civilised society. Once destroyed, the foundations collapse. and of course going against the will of Hashem Who created the heavens and the earth.

TIME TO DEFROST THE FREEZER

There is a common practice in some yeshivos today to make it a precondition of acceptance into the yeshiva that bochurim must agree not to date for a certain period of time (e.g. six months). This is known as "the freezer". I have several concerns about this practice, first and foremost it would seem to be in contradiction to halacha.

Shulchan Aruch (*Even HaEzer*, Siman 1)

Every man is obligated to marry a woman in order to be fruitful and to multiply and anyone who doesn't engage in being fruitful and multiplying is as if he spills blood, And it is as though he is diminishing the [Divine] image, for it is written that in the image of God did He create him, and you shall be fertile and increase. And he causes the Divine Presence to be removed from Israel. And anyone who remains without a wife remains without goodness, without blessing, without a dwelling, without Torah, without a wall, without peace.

The Rem"a adds here:

He who does not marry is not allowed to make a blessing or to engage in Torah etc. and he is not called a man, and when he marries a woman his sins are plugged up, as it is said: "One who has found a wife has found goodness and gains favor in the eyes of God". (Mishlei 18:22)

... It is incumbent on every man that they should marry a woman at the age of 18 and the diligent get married at 13 this mitzvah is for those who choose it, ...but If he is busy with Torah, or if it is too burdensome and he fears to marry a woman in order that he is not burdened in his livelihood and he will not fail in Torah it is permitted to delay.

A few points become apparent from this halacha.

There is a positive mitzvah to marry. This could be delayed if a man fears that the pressures to provide a livelihood would cause him to fail in his Torah study. In the yeshiva world, this is not usually a cause for delay as most bochurim are able to make it a stipulation in their shidduchim that they would like to learn for a certain period after marriage. Kollelim are abound and many girls in the yeshivish world are looking for "learners". So why wait?

It is clear from the Shulchan Aruch that the choice to delay should come from the bochur, and not from any institutions in making this decision, certainly not to make blanket policies.

Rav Chaim Kanievsky would tell bochurim to start looking for a shidduch at age 17 quoting the posuk in *Pirkei Avos* (5:21) "age eighteen to the chuppah" and the Rambam *Hilchos Ishus* (15:2) which states that "the mitzvah to be fruitful and multiply" is incumbent on a man from the age of 17 and if he reaches 20 and has still not made attempts to fulfill this mitzvah, it is as if he transgressed this positive command.

Rav Chaim noted that if yeshivos would end the practice of "the freezer", it would avoid the current "shidduch crisis" by making more bochurim available for marriageable age girls. He was concerned that yeshivos were insisting on "the freezer" more for their own needs than for the needs of the bochurim. (see Naftali Weinberger's biography Rav Chaim p.86).

Does delaying marriage help bochurim? There are a few reasons brought down for not delaying marriage. One is that it prevents children from being brought into the world. The Shulchan Aruch equates this with spilling blood. Particularly in this generation, following the holocaust, and close to the end of days, we must be mindful of the teaching that Moshiach will not come until all neshamas destined to be brought down to this world are born (*Yevamos* 62a).

Another reason that the Torah forbids delaying marriage is that the yetzer hara can overcome unmarried bochurim and bring them to sin. Any rosh yeshiva insisting that they delay marriage could be responsible for leading bachurim to many transgressions.

The Rambam notes (*Hilchos Ishus* 15:3)

> *When a person's soul desires Torah at all times and is obsessed with its [study] as was ben Azzai (see Yevamos 63b), and clings to it throughout his life, without marrying, he is not considered to have transgressed.*

However, it is clear that even in the times of the Gemara, Ben Azai was a remarkable exception. All the more so in our day and age, especially with the added temptations of technology, the majority of yeshiva bochurim in the freezer are clearly at risk from physical urges. Bochurim themselves are the ones best placed to decide if they should seek a wife or not.

Does the "freezer system" result in a high-quality learner? From my perspective, it would seem unfortunately not, which is why I am so opposed to it. I have seen many bochurim coming out of these post-high school yeshivos crying to me that they cannot learn, hence the maggid shiur of a 10th grade who reached out to me for help.

How does a bochur who cannot learn get into such a yeshiva? (Please refer to previous articles). Firstly, a bochur receives a farher, a test on a shtickel Torah and also what they have learned in the previous zman. Since most of the testing is done orally, outside the text, someone with a good memory can remember it by rote, and thus get accepted, even if his textual skills are very weak. They are not asked to translate a posuk in Chumash. There is an assumption that bochurim applying for yeshiva should know how to do this already. But this assumption is wrong. I work with bochurim consistently who have learned in high-level yeshivos, but yet cannot translate a basic posuk from Chumash.

How could a rosh yeshiva, who is not aware of their students' true ability in Torah learning, be equipped to decide if they are ready for marriage or not? I think this problem could be solved if the Rebbeim who test for yeshiva entrance should receive training on how to measure the student's skills, and how to help them if the levels are not up to par.

The job of our yeshivos is to transmit the Torah and the mesorah to the next generation. Period. Once a student reaches marriageable age, it is his job to make sure there is a next generation after him to continue this chain. This is also part of the Torah, as explained above. Pharaoh tried to weaken the Jewish nation by hard labour, but the posuk states "as he inflicted us, so we increased" (*Shemos* 1:12). In the light of recent tragedies in Klal Yisroel where so many Yidden have been lost, we must continue and multiply as the Torah commands.

MAIDSERVANTS, MOTHER: BIRDS AND THE IMPORTANCE OF MESORAH

I received the following question from a teenage girl:

"How could the Torah command a father to sell his daughter into slavery?"

She was referring to the verse in Parshas Mishpatim (*Shemos* 21:7) which states:

וכי־ימכר איש את־בתו לאמה לא תצא כצאת העבדים

Now if a man sells his daughter as a maidservant, she shall not go free as the slaves go free.

She asked: "isn't this cruel? How could the Torah tell a man to sell his daughter with the purpose of the master to marry her. It's disgusting for a 9-year-old girl to get married. This is forced marriage."

I think it is important to address this question. There are many places where the Torah appears to conflict with our modern moral sensibilities. It is vital for all of us, especially parents and educators to understand how to address such questions head-on without dismissing them. When students feel their questions are brushed aside or given only perfunctory answers they feel that maybe the Torah doesn't have all the answers and will start to look elsewhere.

A second reason to address this question is that it shows the supreme importance of not taking the written Torah out of context. It can only be fully understood with the help of the Torah sheb'al peh, the oral Torah, as we shall demonstrate.

The first question we need to address is whether the pasuk is actually referring to a מצות עשה, a positive commandment to sell a daughter. This would seem to hang on how we are to interpret the word כי (ki). Sometimes when a pasuk begins with ki the Torah is meaning "if this happens to you then you will have a mitzvah", suggesting a positive commandment.

For example in Parshas Ki Teitzei (*Devarim* 22:6-7) we read about the mitzvah of Shiluach Haken, sending away the mother bird from the nest. The text reads:

כי יקרא קן־צפור | לפניך בדרך בכל־עץ | או על־הארץ אפרחים או ביצים והאם רבצת על־האפרחים או על־הביצים לא־תקח האם על־הבנים

If a bird's nest chances before you on the road, on any tree or on the ground, [it contains] fledglings or eggs and the mother is sitting upon the fledglings or the eggs, you shall not take the mother upon the young.

שלח תשלח את־האם ואת־הבנים תקח־לך למען ייטב לך והארכת ימים

You shall send away the mother bird, [and then] you may take the young for yourself, in order that it should be good for you, and you should lengthen your days.

The promise of the reward of longevity would seem to suggest that this is a positive commandment. In that case, "ki" does not mean just if you happen upon the nest, and the mother is there and you actually want the eggs or the chicks, you could do it, but rather that there is merit in seeking out opportunities for this mitzvah. (*Aruch Hashulchan* 292:1, *Birchei Yosef* 292:8) quoting the Arizal. Rav Shmuel Kamenetsky (*Am Hatorah Journal* 5:7, pg 12) recommends trying to perform the mitzvah at least once. See, however, *Responsa Chasam Sofer* O.C. 100 and *Responsa Torah Lishmah* 27710. See Responsa Minchas).

Can we apply the same logic to the pasuk regarding selling a daughter as a slave? There is no explicit promise of reward, but the initial "ki" remains the same, potentially indicating a positive mitzvah.

To resolve this question it is necessary to examine our Oral tradition. We do not derive Torah law from logic alone, nor from looking only at the text of the written law. Unlike the ancient Sadducees, Karaites, or the Reform Jews, we do not attempt to derive our religious practices solely from the Written Torah. We have Mesorah, an unbroken chain of tradition passed down together with the written law to Moshe at Har Sinai and transmitted by sages from generation to generation until today. The Torah Sheb'al peh comprises the Mishnah and the Talmud. The Mishnah was compiled between 200–220 CE by Rabbi Yehudah Hanasi. The Gemara is a series of running commentaries and debates concerning the Mishnah. Together, the Mishnah with its relevant Gemaras forms the Talmud.

Even though the Oral Torah was ultimately written down, due to the existential threat of dispersion facing the Jewish civilization following the destruction of the Second Temple in 70 CE, it was written in such as way that it is virtually impossible to understand it without learning it together with a teacher himself steeped in the oral tradition. The belief that at least portions of the Oral Torah were transmitted orally from God to Moshe on Har Sinai during the Exodus from Egypt is a fundamental tenet of faith for religious Jews. Indeed it forms one of the Rambam's Thirteen Principles of Faith, the Ani Maamin recited daily after Shacharis. Many passages of the Torah and the details of laws central to Jewish life are almost incomprehensible without the oral tradition that explains them. They were clearly never meant to be separated, but always learned together.

So let us examine how the oral law explains the pasuk about the father who sells his daughter as a slave. Both the Rambam's Sefer HaMitzvot and the Sefer HaChinuch – compilations of Jewish laws derived from the conclusions of the Talmud and the earlier Torah Law Codes – show that there is no positive commandment at all for one to sell his so daughter even though it states כי. The positive mitzvah is only for the

28

man who buys her as a אמה (maidservant).

In the Rambam's Sefer HaMitzvos, Mitzvah 233 is the mitzvah of ליעד אמה העבריה (liyod ama ivriya) the designation of a Hebrew slave woman. If a Jewish man has acquired a slave woman, he has to marry her or give him as a wife to his son. This mitzvah is derived from the pasuk (*Shemos* 21:8) that "if she is bad in the eyes of her master, who designated her for himself, he must let her be redeemed". Rashi shows, based on a Chazal (*Bechoros* 19a), that this verse hints at the fact of a commandment of designation (marrying her or marrying her off) that precedes the commandment of redemption.

The Rambam goes on to explain that this mitzvah actually shows God's mercy on the poor girl who is sold, and on her father who needed to sell her. In Biblical times, as until very recently, there was no such thing as a girl who could be financially independent. Girls were supported by their fathers or older brothers until they could be married off and supported by a husband. If a father was so poor that he was unable to support his daughter any longer, it was considered a chesed for another family to "buy her": that is, a man would give the father money and in exchange, take the girl in as a member of his household. She would receive work, food, and lodging. Better than redemption is for the master of the house to marry her himself or give her to his son to be married, for this would bring joy to the girl.

The Rambam (*Mishneh Torah* Chapter 4:2 about slaves) explains that a father may only sell his daughter into servitude if he has become so poor that he has nothing left: not land, movables, or even clothing. Even then, as soon as he is able financially, he should be compelled to buy her back to avoid further disgrace to the family. If the father has fled or died or had no means to buy her back, she must serve until she goes free.

Later the Rambam says he cannot force a marriage against the girl's will. She has to be in agreement with the arrangement.

So we see there is no mitzvah to sell a daughter. Rather this is a provision made for a girl whose father was forced to sell her rather than starve to death. What may seem a barbaric practice from the written text alone turns out to be a remarkably compassionate approach when we look at the Mesorah.

IN G-D WE TRUST?
The Supreme Court's acceptance of Toeva Marriages

On Friday June 26 2015 the American people witnessed the fabric of society and the foundation of morality and family life being destroyed. The supreme court of America formally legalised Toeva or same gender marriages, in all 50 states, with the premise of "we can do whatever our "heart" desires, and Hashem will not determine how we should lead our lives."

It is surprising to still see in circulation the American dollar bill with the words "in G-d we trust" emblazoned on each bill, and the President of the United States likewise echoes "G-d bless America" after his speeches to the American people!

The question is, is it Hashem or the Supreme Court they trust?

The US President, who is one of the most influential people in the world, is not setting the tone for justice and moral boundaries, but has now completely damaged the structure of society by formally creating an atmosphere of S'dom and Amorrah.

The rainbow emblem of Toeva relationships, which represents openly and accepted permissiveness, is now splashed all over America with flags and even rainbow colored lights which were shone over the

White House in celebration of the new legislation. This rainbow symbol, which personifies rebelliousness "against" Hashem's will, actually epitomises the opposite in the Torah.

After the Mabul, Hashem made a covenant with Noach, that He would never flood the world again and whenever the Satan would accuse and condemn mankind, Hashem would bring a rainbow to remind us of the covenant with Noach. Therefore, when the rainbow appears, it is to assure us that despite our aveiros, Hashem promises not to bring destruction again. This consideration when seeing the rainbow should invoke teshuva in mankind's hearts and minds.

Today's world transmits the opposite message. The rainbow colors are now representing the opposite of Hashem's will through perversion and immorality.

We can look back to the tremendous foresight of the Lubavitcher Rebbe ZT"L, when, over 3 decades ago, in 1981, he foresaw the rapid decline of morality and thus created a campaign to teach the Seven Mitzvos Bnei Noach to mankind. In fact, the President at that time, President Ronald Reagan, backed the Rebbe's call to educate the masses and to maintain morality in the world. With this in mind, on April 4, 1982, the National Day of Reflection was born.

Clearly, unfortunately, whilst there are those upstanding citizens who do adhere to the Seven Mitzvos Bnei Noach, the mandates are not fully integrated into our society, as can be seen from the latest developments of Toeva marriages, which is one of the 7 Noachide Laws.

With the above elucidated for us, what should our goal be now?

Klal Yisroel is considered "a light unto the nations" (*Yeshaya* 42:6), and we are obligated to act as an example to the world, and beseech Hashem for the Supreme court to re-track this law of abomination. As the Lubavitcher Rebbe proclaimed through foresight, in order to regenerate the foundations of morality, we need to continue educating the masses to the significance of keeping the Mitzvos Bnei Noach and strengthen the already existing groups.

Just as Asifas have taken place acting as prevention against the pitfalls of internet usage, we need to create an awareness in our establishments to educate our children, that, even though pervasiveness has unfortunately become allowed and accepted in the wider society as normal, it remains not just "ossur min haTorah" (*Vayikra* 20:13), it is ossur for all mankind, through the Seven Mitzvos Bnei Noach.

May "in G-d we trust" manifest itself in its true sense, where all mankind will accept that Hashem Hu HaElokim, Hashem Echad.

Bris Milah: Identifying the Real Deal

Abraham was commanded by God to circumcise himself and his descendants. As the ספר החינוך brings down, the mitzvah of ברית מילה is stated in Parshas Lech Lecha (*Bereishis* 17:11) and again in Parshas Tazriah (*Vayikra* 12:3). The root of the mitzvah, he explains, is to be a sign, distinguishing the bodies of the Jewish males, from those of the non-Jews. Just as our souls are different, so we will have a sign to show how our bodies are different too. Just as Hashem's plan for the Jew is to perfect the form of his soul through his actions in this world, so too, we perfect our bodies through this mitzvah.

Rabbeinu Bachya writes in כד הקמה in chapter מילה, Abraham was promised that his descendants would receive three מתנות from Hashem for fulfilling the mitzvah of ברית מילה:

מלכות בית דוד would never cease.

ארץ ישראל will be given to his descendants forever.

The Divine Presence will rest among the Jewish people.

Yet we find that the Arabs and many non-Jews circumcise themselves. If so, how is circumcision serving as a unique distinguishing physical feature of the Jew? The question is even stronger when we look at the Rambam in הלכות מלכים פ"י:ח

אמרו חכמים שבני קטורה שהם זרעו של אברהם שבא אחר ישמעאל ויצחק חייבין במילה. והואיל ונתערבו היום בני ישמעאל בבני קטורה יתחייבו הכל במילה בשמיני

34

Our Sages have said that the sons of Keturah, those who are the De-
scendents of Abraham who came after Ishmael and Isaac, are obli-
gated with the mitzvah of ברית מילה. *However, today, since the De-*
scendents of Ishmael have commingled with the children of Keturah,
all of them are obligated with ברית מילה *on the eighth day.*

So it appears today there is no difference between the Jews and Arabs. Both are commanded to perform ברית מילה on themselves.

This clearly contradicts what we learn from the Sefer HaChinuch.
How can we resolve this apparent conflict in opinions?

The מנחת חינוך offers an answer to this question. The main mitzvah
of ברית מילה is פריעה which uncovers the skin by removing the thin
membrane beneath the foreskin:

הנה בודאי פריעה הוא מגוף המצוה כמבואר בשבת פר"א דמילה מל ולא פרע
כאילו ....לא מל לשיטת הרמב"ם מה' מלכים דבני קטורה חייבים עתה ג"כ
במילה. אינם חייבין רק במילה ולא בפריעה כיון דהוא הלכה למשה מסיני והלכה
למשה מסיני לא נאמרה רק לישראל לבד......אם כן נהי דבני קטורה חייבים דהם
זרעו של אאע"ה אינם חייבין רק במילה ולא בפריעה כנלע"ד

Behold for sure פריעה is the main part of the mitzvah as it explains
in the Gemara Shabbos פר"א that circumcision without פריעה is considered as if no circumcision took place, according to the opinion of
the Rambam in מה' מלכים that the sons of Keturah are obligated also for
circumcisions they are obligated just for circumcision, not פריעה since
פריעה is הלכה למשה מסיני, and הלכה למשה מסיני was only said to the Jewish
people it comes that out although the sons of Keturah are obligated for
circumcision because they are from the seeds of Abraham they are only
obligated for the circumcision not for פריעה this is how it appears to me.

If we take this approach, then the actual mitzvah given uniquely to
the Jews is not the procedure of circumcision per se, which is done the
world over for both religious and health reasons, but rather פריעה as
given to us as הלכה למשה מסיני. The obligation of the Arabs mentioned
by the Rambam is simply circumcision, removing the foreskin.

The Arabs only do a partial ברית. Superficially it looks very similar to
ours but it is not. It is more like a Chinese imitation of a designer brand.

To the outsider, the two may be indistinguishable but to those in the know, the imitation lacks certain features and is of far lesser value.

We have the complete sign of what Hashem wants us to do. However, since the Arabs have a partial mitzvah of ברית מילה, they are still rewarded. What is their reward?

Rabbi Novick brings down in his Sefer "Fascinating Torah Prophecies" pages 53-56 the Zohar (11 32a) ויהב להו חולקא לתתא בארעא קדישא בנין ההוא נזירו דבהון וזמינין בני ישמעאל למשלט בארעא קדישא כד איתי ריקניא מכלא זמנא כמה דגזירו דלהון בדיקיא בלא שלימו

Hashem will give the Arabs control over ארץ ישראל because of the bris. And it will be that Arabs will rule over ארץ ישראל while it is barren just as their bris is barren and not completed.

As mentioned above, the purpose of ברית מילה it is to perfect our souls. It is a lifelong struggle to reach this closeness to God as it states (Iyov 5:7) כי־אדם לעמל יולד – a man is born to labor.

Maybe that could be the reason at the time of the circumcision we say:

כשם שנכנס לברית כן יכנס לתורה לחופה ולמעשים טובים

Just like he entered the bris, so shall he enter for Torah, the chuppah (wedding canopy), and the good deeds.

He enters into the ברית to reach the highest level of perfection that is humanly possible. How does he achieve this? Learning Torah brings a man closer to Hashem to serve him with happiness. True happiness depends on marriage as the Gemara (*Yevamoth* 63b) says the ultimate happiness a person can experience in this world is dependent upon marriage.

אמר רבי תנחום א"ר חנילאי כל אדם שאין לו אשה שרוי בלא שמחה בלא ברכה בלא טובה בלא שמחה דכתיב (דברים יד, כו) ושמחת אתה וביתך בלא ברכה דכתיב (יחזקאל מד, ל) להניח ברכה אל ביתך בלא טובה דכתיב (בראשית ב, יח) לא טוב היות האדם לבדו

Rabbi Tanḥum said that Rabbi Ḥanilai said: Any man who does not have a wife is left without happiness without blessing, without

goodness.

And of course, a truly happy marriage is dependent on a lifetime of good deeds, thinking about the other and not himself.

Spiritual closeness in the physical world requires the removal of a physical barrier: ברית מילה. The בית אלהים (p.8) expounds a remarkably deep concept regarding the ברית מילה.

וזו היא הוראת המילה ביום השמיני ללידתו,לומר שלא נברא האדם להתנהג על טבע העולם כבעלי חיים אלא לטרוח לפעול פעוליו מכוינות ליוצרו. ולהחליש בידיו דבר המביאו לידי עבירה,והיא הערלה,וביוסב השמיני ימול בשר ערלתו,להורות כי בזה יהיה גובר על טבע העולם,שהם שבעת הימים, ששת ימי המעשה ויום השביעי שנברא למנוחה,ואם כן האדם כולל המלכים שהם במדרגה עליונה, והבעלי חיים שהם במדרגה תחתונה

This is to teach us regarding the ברית מילה *which is performed on the 8th day of the childbirth to say that a person is not created to accustom himself to the physical nature of the world — animalistic instincts solely for pleasure — but rather bother himself with his whole being to one who formed him (Hashem) and to weaken the thing which causes one to sin that is a foreskin on the 8th day he is circumcised of his foreskin to teach with this. Only by cutting off the foreskin can one be victorious over the nature of the world (Lust) which is 7 days (6 days were the days of creation and on the seventh day Hashem created rest). If so, man is in the category of* מלכים *which is the level of Heaven spirituality as opposed to animalistic lust which is the level of the physical world.*

So cutting off the foreskin and completing the mitzvah with פריעה is the only way to achieve that spiritual closeness to Hashem in this physical world. In essence, true Bris Milah is a spiritual procedure. Hence the Kitzur Shulchan Aruch (קיצור שולחן ערוך ה:טו) who points out that whilst it is forbidden to say brachos or divrei Torah in the presence of nakedness, bris milah (where the baby is uncovered) is an exception. But why? It is still nakedness. Maybe one can answer that ברית מילה is a spiritual procedure even though it appears physical. As the בית יוסף writes in the טור יורה דעה סימן רוח

מביא הראש שכתב וגם נראה דכיון דלתקוני המילה קא אתי הרינו ביה שפיר והיה
מחניך קדוש ואין בו אותו שעה משום לא יראה בך ערות דבר (דברים כ"ג טו)

The בית יוסף brings down the Rosh who writes that since he is completing the circumcision it is called "and so your camp shall be holy" and it is not at that moment "He will not see in you nakedness".

The Rosh wants to teach us that even though ברית מילה may appear nakedness, since you are completing the spiritual aspect at that moment פריעה, it is purely holy therefore one can make a blessing in front of the baby fully uncovered. It is called והיה מחניך קדוש "and so your camp shall be holy".

In this way, the Jews are distinguished from the non-Jews. Even though their circumcisions may physically resemble ours, they remain physical procedures, whereas ours are spiritual ones.

PART TWO:
ANCIENT PERSPECTIVES ON CURRENT EVENTS

CORONAVIRUS BRINGING THE LESSON HOME

The Coronavirus has shocked the world. All the yeshivos and schools have been shut down. The menahalim, rebbeim and teacher's have no jobs and they are struggling to keep the students engaged armed only with a phone line or using Zoom. Such a thing has never happened in the history of the Jewish people. Even during the Roman Occupation when it was illegal to teach Torah, Rabbi Akiva went ahead and taught Torah anyway. He defied the ban. A Jew without learning is like a fish out of water. Even the threat to our physical existence was not as concerning as the spiritual threat incurred by a universal abandonment of teaching. So Rabbi Akiva taught, ultimately sacrificing his physical life to preserve the spiritual existence of the Jewish people.

My Gateshead education instilled in me the hashkafah that all Torah learning protects from diseases. The Gemara in Shabbos 119b quotes Reish Lakish as saying " The world exists only in the merit of the breath that comes out of school children". Why theirs specifically? Because their breath is pure, untainted by sin. The Maharsha their says since the world's existence depends on untainted Torah learning, it is especially dependent on children's learning. In light of this we would expect the yeshivos to be increasing their hours rather than closing their doors. The Steipler Gaon ztz"l would point out how accidents in Eretz Yisroel increase during Bein Hazmanim because the decreased learning leads to decreased shemirah. In a similar vein the Gemara (*Shabbos* 119b) states that if one answers "Amen, yehei shemei rabbah" with all his might, punishments and decrees will be torn up. Yet, due to the current situation, we are prevented from gathering in minyanim to recite the Kaddish.

We are baffled by the current situation. The *Halacha itself* forbids davening in a shul or teaching in a school, lest it cause a person to die. One who goes ahead anyway is considered a murderer or a rodef? Shuls, kollelim, yeshivos and Beis yaakovs throughout the world stand empty. Clearly this is a gezeira min hashamoyim. Yet our usual weapons for reversing the decrees are withheld. How can we understand this? Undoubtedly the world is changing for the good. Nations are being forced to work together in harmony. It is hard to imagine we and the world will not be transformed by this experience. But whatever good emerges how can we understand why the yeshivos, even the elite ones are empty?

As Rav Mendel Kessin point out, there is no prophecy today, but Chazal tell us that a chacham can in a way be better than a prophet. A prophet can only reveal that which was revealed to him, but a chacham can use implications and deductions to get a better grasp of what is going on. So we turn to the words of Chazal to shed light on this worldwide catastrophe.

In Parshas Noach (*Bereishis* 6:12-13) Rashi says on the phrase "all the flesh had corrupted" that even domestic animals, beasts and birds had relations with animals outside of their species. Regarding the "end of all flesh" Rashi, quoting the Midrash Tanchuma explains wherever promiscuity and idol worship catastrophe will come into the world destroying the good and the bad. We might therefore surmise that Coronavirus, which is surely causing devastation on a completely global scale, is brought upon the world due to the sexual immorality that abounds in our current culture. If this were the case, the "good and bad" might be destroyed. Tzaddikim could get sick. But again this does not explain to us the particularly perplexing question of why the doors of the Shuls and the yeshivos should close? If Hashem were angered by immorality surely Torah should be the antidote?

We know that when Hashem brings challenges of this magnitude, it is a punishment, or at least a wake up call to the Jewish people (*Yevamos* 33a), and that Hashem operates middah kneged middah (*Sanhedrin* 90a). What actions have we committed that are causing Hashem to close yeshivos? To the extent that opening them might render us murderers?

Why are the yeshivos closed? If the hockey team suddenly starts losing in the middle of the season, they sack the coach. Could the reason for the yeshivos closing their doors be something to do with how the yeshivos are operating? Perhaps this is a wake up call.

Although we might think that prior to Coronavirus, yeshivos were resounding with the pure, happy sound of children learning Torah, unfortunately this is not the complete picture. In my work, I teach the children who are in public school because no yeshiva or Beis Yaakov would accept them. For them the doors of the schools were always closed. I see the former Kolleleit who were never taught the basics of grammar in Lashon haKodesh and so struggle in their learning and lose enthusiasm. I see the Ba'alei teshuvah who leave yeshivos because no one can teach them the fundamental skills they need to get truly caught up to their peers in learning.

I hear about the rebbeim who cannot teach but cannot be fired because of protektzia or because their family needs the parnassa, meanwhile the students suffer in ways that can seriously affect their connection to yiddishkeit. I hear about the girls who cry because they cannot get into seminary. I hear about the 12 year old boys, overwhelmed and terrified because they must take a farher in five different schools. What are we doing to our precious Jewish neshamos?

Of course the rebbeim are overworked and underpaid, the yeshivos are bursting at the seams struggling to find spaces for all the students and to balance their budgets. Each school aims to outdo its competitor in terms of material covered. Now they are valiantly struggling to keep the students learning through teleconferences, it is a logistical nightmare. But perhaps instead of adding for phone classes, this should be a time for deep reflection. Is this system working? Are yeshivos succeeding in instilling the next generation with a love of Torah, Yiddishkeit and the tools to succeed in learning?

Yeshivos have a spiritual responsibility for the neshamos of every child. A proper foundation in aleph Beis and skills for learning will help children feel success in their learning and motivated to try harder, instead of the students I so frequently see who became disillusioned simply because their educational needs were not met. Children should not be excluded because they do not fit the mould. Children should not be given homework so that even the home becomes a battleground instead of a warm respite at the end of the day.

So many children have experienced the doors of Torah learning closed in their face. Now the doors of yeshivos are closed to everyone. They are closed to the top bachur and to the weakest student, the troublemakers with ADHD and the best behaved, the rich kids and the poor ones, yeshivish, chareidi, modern. Coronavirus does not distinguish.

Maybe it's time to say every kid can get accepted into a school we will be Zoche for moshiach to come and Machla taken away.

SAFETY MEASURES TO PREVENT THE SPREAD OF "DIS-AFFECTION"

With the start of the new zman, students across the world are returning to their learning institutions with many safety measures in place to prevent the transmission of COVID. Masks, hand sanitiser, plexiglass screens, quarantine, social distancing: these protocols are being put in place to protect the community from Coronavirus and also to prevent the schools from being shut down by the government for non-compliance.

As frum Jews, however, we must remember that it wasn't the virus or the government that caused the recent lockdown; it was Hashem. Hashem shut down all the Jewish institutions around the world. What did we do wrong that Hashem closed us down? What תשובה do we need to do?

In my previous articles, I argued that the coronavirus is a wake-up call to all of us. If Hashem closed down the schools, maybe we have to change the system. Too many children are being lost each year to Yiddishkeit because of problems with the educational system. Just as we are willing to make very drastic changes to ensure the physical safety of our kids, minimise the spread of Infection and avoid a government shutdown, so we need to put in place measures to ensure the spiritual safety of our kids, minimise the spread of disaffection and avoid a further Divine shutdown. We have to enable every child, regardless of his or her ability, to find Simcha in Torah learning and enjoy the chinuch experience so that no student will be left behind. Here are 17 suggestions for achieving this.

1) It is the responsibility of the school to teach Alef Bais in a manner that all children will be reading effortlessly and fluently. This skill has to be implemented primarily before studying Nikudos (vowels).

2) When teaching the **Letters** and **Nekudos,** this method should be taught **according to our Mesorah,** keeping it simple, using the methodology handed down through the generations. First, we teach the fluency of naming the letters, followed by "Kometz, Alef, Aa".

Unfortunately, too many children are being taught using phonic sounds and cute pictures. This may appear to be the modern and more effective method of teaching but this derech has seeped in from the non-Jewish approach. Using phonic sounds instead of identifying the actual letter, it will appear that the student is reading, but he is actually just sounding out the syllables within the word, not seeing the word itself. Eventually, he will struggle with translation and Rashi reading.

3) After the student has been taught the skill of reading Hebrew, he should receive periodical testing, checking that his accuracy and fluency level in school is maintained throughout his elementary years. **No biblical Hebrew** taught until the student is **fluent in Hebrew** reading. because they will be reading in syllables, not in whole words, and will not be able to distinguish between the roots of the words or prefix or suffix, since they only see random letters together, but not the root of the word.

4) When learning to translate, students must learn to **translate clearly into their mother tongue.** When an English translation is interspersed with many Yiddish or Yeshivish terms, students need to expend much extra brain energy to decipher such a linguistically complex mixture, usually resulting in lack of attention, loss of focus, and a lack of clarity and incomprehension.

The phenomenon arises because rebbeim feel they are carrying on a Mesorah. Unfortunately, this is not a Mesorah, as we see from Moshe Rabbeinu who gave over the Torah in 70 languages so that no one could say they didn't understand the Torah. Torah must be taught in the language which the student understands. I have witnessed many students burning out because they did not learn in their mother tongue. Even when it appears the student is reading and translating fluently in Yiddish, it doesn't mean he actually understands what he is saying.

5. When learning a text, a student should be able to read fluently, translate exactly, understand the context, and explain the sentence structure, whether it is Chumash or Gemara. He must learn how to add extra words to explain the sentences, since Chumash and Gemara are very concise, unlike English or any other language which can be understood right away. Consequently, this ability will enable the student to be able to learn on his own. If a student is unable to do this, it is a clear sign that the requisite skills for learning are not yet in place. The pressure to cover material should never come at the expense of fundamental skills which are most important for being able to enjoy learning and to learn independently beyond Yeshiva.

6. The student must be able to read **fluently before starting Chumash.** The minimum a student should know is the Chumshei Torah first before starting Mishnayos. Teaching Gemara should only start at the age of 15 and later as it is clearly stated in שולחן ערוך אבן העזר סימן א סעיף ג:

מצוה על כל אדם ש יש א אשה בן י״ח. באר היטב כתב שם אע״ג דכל המצות חייב לקיים מיד כשנגעשה הבן י״ג מ״מ מצוה זו קבלו חכמינו ז״ל שבן י״ח לחופה מאחר שצריך ללמוד קודם שישא אשה התחלת לימוד גמרא הוא מבן ט״ו ואילך

Institutions teaching Gemara to students before 15 years old are clearly going against halacha as the באר היטב wrote. **All those institutions that teach Gemara under the age of 15 years old must stop this practice.**

Before commencing Gemara, the minimum should be knowing all the Mesechtas of Mishnayos which are required for the Yeshiva system, plus Nach inside until Melachim.

7. It is crucial that **rebbeim should use consistent pronunciation throughout the school system**. I have met many talmidim over the years whose learning suffered because of the confusion generated by inconsistencies in pronunciation.

8. Children should not be pressured to absorb more than they are capable of at their specific age. Concerning homework, I would like to quote my Rebbi, **Rav Mattisyahu Salomon, who advocates a no-homework policy. "School should be the place to learn and the home should be a place of refuge and time with the family."** (With Hearts Full of Love, Artscroll/Mesorah. P. 79-83). Any institution which does not follow his words " no homework policy" is going against daas Torah and should be shut down.

9) **Medicating a student is the last resort, and never addresses underlying causes of academic issues**. It is a crutch used by many institutions to eliminate extra expenses of remediation and hence behavioral issues. A senior Rosh HaYeshiva confided to me that, in their community, medication has been used for over 3 generations. From my experience, I have seen that children who are unfocused in class and labeled ADD/ADHD, most probably have underdeveloped academic skills that have not been diagnosed, which will ultimately create disinterest in the classroom, leading to a lack of understanding of the material presented by the teacher. Other factors that could present as ADD/ADHD are sleep deprivation, too much junk food (white sugar, processed foods, etc.), skipping breakfast, lack of exercise to name a few.

9. Educators must consider the possibility that an unsuccessful child might be a victim of some sort of abuse (physical, mental, emotional, or sexual) which is, unfortunately, a growing problem in our communities.

10) **All educators in frum schools/yeshivos including rebbeim and Menahelim should be required to enroll in some form of kiruv program before starting classroom placements to learn how to transmit Torah teachings and values with Simcha and positivity.**

11) Communication and respect between parents and the Hanhala are crucial. Whilst the educator has the premier responsibility of the child's education during school, **a parent's requests should be taken into consideration.**

12) Jewish hashkafa should be emphasised in school. **Hashkafa provides the grounding of how a Yid should live and serve Hashem properly and that Hashem loves all of us.** It should be noted that children can not be expected to accept everything they hear from the rebbi without being allowed to ask questions. Questions are a natural way that children learn and clarify concepts. Children should not be made to feel that they are questioning the validity of the Torah chas v'shalom.

13) As in my previous articles, I advocate **never to expel a student from an institution** without having a plan B put in place. A child simply rejected from the Yeshiva system will feel anger and resentment towards Hashem and this is very dangerous. If the menahel feels the child would be better suited for a different type of institution, it is his responsibility to find the child a suitable alternative and to explain to the child how it would be to his benefit. This way the child can feel he has options and can make a choice that is in his best interests. If the child refuses to leave, then the menahel needs to seek advice on how to deal with him. HaRav Steinman זצ"ל gave a rebuke to a menahel when asked if a menahel should accept a certain child whom he felt was not "their type" for his school. He answered back that this philosophy was merely Gaava and that all children should be accepted.

14) **Never punish a student by writing out a Gemara as retribution for not following the place.** I have worked with many adults who won't learn certain Gemaras until this day since they had been administered that Masechta as a punishment as a child. It should go without saying that there is no place for hitting the student or throwing him out of the classroom.

15) Tefilla is crucial. A student must learn the translation and understand what he is saying, otherwise davening will become boring and meaningless.

16) The rebbi is the key in making a student's experience in school the most memorable and uplifting experience. **Parnasa should never be a criteria for keeping a poor Mechanech employed in a school or Yeshiva if it means putting children at risk.**

17) **All children/bochurim or girls should never be refused acceptance** or put on trial for the month to see if he/she"fits in" to which every Jewish institution they apply too. Let us remember Hitler, may his name be blotted out, murdered 2 million Jewish children in the Holocaust, we cannot let that happen again. By refusing with excuses such as "we are too full" or "the child does not fit into our mold" or "we do not have the resources to help your son/daughter". In my decades of experience, institutions always find money for what they need.

As we prepare for the new school year with COVID-19 safety protocols in place, let us also remember these spiritual safety strategies to ensure our children stay focused and motivated and learn with Simcha. This will drastically reduce the risk of disaffection and defection.

FREEDOM CONVOY 2022

Everything that happens in this world is orchestrated by Hashem. All events ultimately prepare us for the arrival of Moshiach. Although our Prophets and sages have described for us changes in the world that will herald the coming of Moshiach, the actual timing is hidden from us.

Recently we witnessed the Convoy of truckers, protesting vaccine mandates, that started in Canada becoming a movement spread over the entire world. What does this have to do with the coming of Moshiach?

There is a famous Gemara in *Sotah* 49b which describes the times heralding the approach of Moshiach.

One of these famous signs is: פני הדור כפני הכלב "the face of the generation will be like the face of a dog".

As Rabbi Yisrael Salanter *ztz"l* explained: A dog by nature runs ahead of its master, always turning around to see where he is heading; and whatever that direction may be, the dog arrives there first. The phrase *pnei hador* ("the face of the generation") often signifies those who are [supposed to be] the leaders of the generation. In our days, we see how our leaders are leaders only in name. They spend their time looking around to see where their people would like to head, and they run there first…

The whole world can see how our so-called leaders are fulfilling this prophecy פני הדור כפני הכלב. They are removing the mandate gradually, because of the truckers, and hopefully they will eventually succeed because these superficial leaders merely look back like a כלב to see where their people would like to head, and they run there first…

In the second part of עלינו לשבח we recite:

וכל בני בשר יקראו בשמך, להפנות אליך כל רשעי ארץ, יכירו וידעו כל יושבי תבל
כי לך תכרע כל ברך תשבע כל לשון

And all mankind will invoke Your Name, to turn back to You, all the wicked of the earth. They will realise and know, all the inhabitants of the world, that to You, every knee must bend, every tongue must swear [allegiance to You].

I always wondered how it would happen that all mankind would turn towards Hashem. It doesn't say in the prayer that we Jews would cause it to happen but rather it just will happen as Hashem told us in *Beshalach* (14:14).

ה' ילחם לכם ואתם תחרשון

"Hashem will fight for you, but you shall remain silent."

We are assured that there will be a unity amongst different countries, people and cultures that כל בני בשר "a unified mankind" יקראו בשמך "will invoke Your name".

How will it happen?

Where will it start?

Maybe this invoking of Hashem's name is starting in Ottawa Canada. I went down there with my family to see the true story of the truckers with my own eyes. The media and the government here in Canada calls them nazis and terrorists. What I witnessed first hand however was a united group of peace-loving people. One speaker took the stage. Addressing the crowds he said "we are all immigrants from different backgrounds, but we are all Canadian citizens. We have a constitution: God-given rights and freedom in this country. Let us unite and take away this evilness and bring back our freedom". On the side of a truck stationed in front of Parliament I saw verses in English from Yeshaya chapter (55:6)

Seek the Lord when He is found, call Him when He is near.

The wicked shall give up his way, and the man of iniquity his thoughts, and he shall return to the Lord, Who shall have mercy upon him, and to our God, for He will freely pardon.

We recite these verses on Yom Kippur, the holiest day of the year Yom Kippur in the amidah of Neilah. Where? In אתה הבדלת "You set man apart" - the climax of the Amidah. I was humbled by this call to repentance in the midst of the awesome sight of the demonstrations.

The Canadian founder of Adopt-a-Trucker, Chris Garral said in an interview with Fox News "I feel God's behind us" When asked about his attitude towards prime minister Trudeau he replied "I'm very sorry for him. I pray for him that he turns his heart and repents…" Surprising sentiments from this so-called "terrorist". Remarkably the words echo the prophecies of Yechezkel (18:23)

החפץ אחפץ מות רשע נאם אדני ה' הלוא בשובו מדרכיו וחיה

Do I desire the death of the wicked? says the Lord God. Is it not rather in his repenting of his ways that he may live? (This verse is also in אתה הבדלת).

The Gentiles are turning their hearts to Hashem as our sages predicted in the gemara ועל מה יש לנו להשען על אבינו שבשמים And upon what is there for us to rely? Only upon our Father in heaven. And on that day והיה ה' למלך על כל הארץ ביום ההוא יהיה ה' אחד ושמו אחד on that day, Hashem will be One and His Name One.

We should follow in the footsteps of the peace-loving Canadian Convoy 2022 and rectify the sin of שנאת חינם "baseless hatred" - hatred of others for no real reason that caused our בית המקדש to be destroyed, and the Jewish people to be in exile for close to 2,000 years.

Amazingly this Convoy started in the month of Adar – a time of eradicating evil as it states clearly in the prayer following the megillah reading. פיהם פתחו כל יושב תבל כי פור המן נהפך לפורנו All the people in the world open their mouth to praise Hashem because Haman's chosen day to destroy us was turned upside-down and became our cause for celebration.

The convoy took place around the time of Purim, a time of eradicating evil from the world. At the same time protesters were invoking pesukim from Yom Kippur about universal repentance. The Vilna Gaon points out that the word "purim" is found in the biblical name for Yom Kippur – Yom haki-PURIM – which means "a day like Purim." That which we accomplish on Yom Kippur with spiritual pursuits, we accomplish on Purim with physical pursuits.

We might assume Yom Kippur is the greater of the two days. But in one sense, Purim is even greater. It is easier to achieve spiritual elevation on a day like Yom Kippur, when we pray and have no time for forbidden activities like gossip or getting angry. By fasting, the soul achieves dominance over the body. But on Purim, in our state of rambunctious inebriation, it is much harder to maintain our human dignity. In this way, the challenge of Purim is greater. That's why, by comparison, Yom hakiPurim is only "a day like Purim."

I would like to end off with a blessing that the convoys should go from strength to strength in eradicating the evilness of the governments around the world who are limiting freedoms.

AN ICE STORM STORY

We all have inspirational stories we can share with one another. Let me share with you a short story which happened to me this past week.

Montreal is well known for its harsh winters, even in late February and last week was no exception. We experienced one of our infamous ice storms. It's actually a beautiful sight to behold, everything in its path covered with a glistening layer of ice, as if turned to glass. The downside is, that very often the power lines are covered with ice too and in this case it created a blackout around 11 PM.

Just before this happened, we had a medical emergency in the family, and ended up rushing to the local hospital. Boruch Hashem everything ended up fine in the end, but we had to spend the night there waiting for the doctor. At 5:30 AM I called home to find out if we had power yet but my son told me that the street was still in complete darkness. I was concerned as I was scheduled to learn with a student online from England at 6:10 AM and I had no way of contacting him to cancel the session since my cell would not allow me to call out of State. Boruch Hashem we were released at 5:50 AM which would give me enough time to get home to teach if the power were to go on.

I talked to Hashem to please restore power so that I could teach the student at 6:10am. We arrived home at 6:00 AM and still had no electricity. Before I got out of my car I prayed again for power, as this bochur was really shteiging now and would be very disappointed that

54

we wouldn't. Just when I finished praying, the lights went on. In fact it was just enough time for my computer to reboot. I was ready to teach at 6:10 AM.

This story really inspired me. Even though we know Hashem has His time when to answer our tefillos, I got the message that for Hashem, Torah learning is a priority! I just had to reach out to Him.

Don't worry, the story doesn't end here. That Friday night after Maariv, I told my friend what had happened to me earlier that week. He seemed shocked. He told me that he has a sleep apnea machine, which his doctor instructed him to use every night. The night of the ice storm, he couldn't fall asleep because there was no electricity for his machine. He kept checking the Hydro Quebec Information Line to discover the time the lights were scheduled to go back on. He said that it explicitly stated on the website that they were only going on at 7:30 AM and not before. But he said "because of Torah learning, the lights had to go on!!!"

Two ideas were displayed to me as Chazal teach us. Firstly, Hashem answers even the most simplest prayer. Secondly, the whole purpose of this world is to teach and learn Torah.

CONVERSATION WITH A PASTOR

In addition to my new book "I CAN Learn" from Feldheim, I offer a free book called "Struggling with Hebrew Reading, Frustrated in Torah Learning" which is a compilation of articles that have been published over the years about the program. Of course, this material is geared toward the Torah learning community, so I was taken aback to receive an order for 10 copies from a certain gentleman named "Jerome Garcia" (actual name changed), but suffice to say it didn't sound like a Jewish name I was curious what he might want with my book.

On the other hand, perhaps he was a ger tzedek, in which case it would make perfect sense that he was struggling with Hebrew reading. I would have been more than happy to send him copies of my book to help him and his friends. As I was in a quandary, I figured I will start by asking him which (if any) shul he affiliates with and I emailed him the next morning.

It turned out that Mr Garcia was a pastor in the States, a born-again "Judeo Christian" and leader of the "Chosen Flock" congregation (name also changed but you get the idea). I offered to send instead material about the seven Noahide laws which it is obligated for all non-Jews to follow and which, I assured him, would be very "cleansing for the soul".

As an aside, here are the seven Noachide laws: Take a look and see for yourselves if you think the Gentiles in the year 2023 are measuring up to Hashem's expectations of them.

1 Do not profane G-d's Oneness in any way.

2 Do not curse your Creator.

3 Do not murder.

4 Do not eat a limb of a still-living animal.

5 Do not steal.

6 Do not be sexually immoral.

7 Establish courts of law and ensure justice in our world.

Jerome Garcia, it seemed, however, was not interested in the Noachide laws. In fact, he tried to convince me that Yoshka was the messiah, citing Yechezkel as a source for all the supposed indications of his messianic status. Of course, all the things he quoted were misquoted and mistranslated, and taken completely out of context, in order to fit in with their well-known but misguided narrative. Of the two of us, who is in a better position to understand the meaning and intent of passages from Tanach? If he was able to read Yechezkel, Yeshaya, and the like in the original Hebrew with meforshim, he wouldn't have been ordering 10 copies of my book. So what could he tell me what those texts are actually saying? How ironic that I, a rabbi – who has published a book to help people read Hebrew and learn Torah – should be told what the bible is really saying by a man who cannot even read that bible in its original language.

I would assume that my readership does not need a blow-by-blow account of exactly where the Christians went wrong and how they distorted our texts. But I think two important lessons for all of us can be brought out from this interchange.

The first is that it should not be beyond anyone with a Torah education to be able to read the Novi in the original language, look at the meforshim and see for themselves what these texts say. If that is beyond your abilities, you need to work on these skills, as I advocate in my book. These are the skills needed for independent learning.

Unlike in Judaism where every rabbi – indeed every Torah Jew – is by definition a scholar, Christian leaders are rarely scholars. Most of them cannot read Hebrew (hence this pastor trying to order my book!!). A friend of mine recently met a completely illiterate pastor, he couldn't even read the bible in English (his mother tongue)! Most are simply charismatic, inspirational leaders, or just well-meaning caring types. Even those rare Christian scholars who can read and translate Hebrew, do not look at the Rashi or other commentaries. Yet it is not always possible, even with a correct translation, to understand the meaning of passages from Tanach without meforshim. Chazal and the meforshim had an encyclopedic knowledge of Tanach that enabled them to see each pasuk in its true context and we can and must rely on their understanding to elucidate these passages.

It might be beyond your average gentile pastor, but it shouldn't be beyond a yeshiva-educated bachur. Knowledge is power. The best way to defeat missionaries is to make sure we and our kids are well-armed with skills so that they can make mincemeat of any "argument".

If anyone is interested in learning more about the missionaries' arguments and how to defeat them, I recommend a two-volume series by Rabbi Tovia Singer "Let's Get Biblical: Why Doesn't Judaism Accept the Christian Messiah", which gives an in-depth analysis and refutation of all missionary arguments. I also encouraged Mr Garcia to visit Rabbi Singer's website outreachjudaism.org for answers to the various questions he was sending me.

The second point that should be made is that if a non-Jew seeking to bring Jews and non-Jews closer to his religion is going to the trouble of ordering and reading a book to improve Hebrew reading and upgrade his Torah learning skills, then kal v'chomer (all the more so), frum Jews, for whom Torah learning is our main occupation, should do the same.

Christianity, the world's largest religion, is based on fundamental translation mistakes. More than two and a half billion people today (and many more throughout history) have been duped because they cannot read Hebrew texts and understand them, a mistake they will surely regret at the end of days.

I noted to Mr. Garcia that it was perhaps not insignificant that he wanted to order ten copies of my book. Ten is a significant number. I pointed out to him that at the end of time, the Gentiles will look for the truth. The great prophet Zechariah (8:23) prophesied at the end of days, "So said the Lord of Hosts: In those days, that ten men of all the languages of the nations will take hold of the skirt of a Jewish man, saying, "Let us go with you, for we have heard that God is with you."

But we, the Jewish people, are far fewer in number. There are a mere 16 million worldwide which means for every one Jew in the world there are over 162 Christians. Of those Jews, according to statistics in the US, less than 20 percent of them keep kosher, and probably far fewer are what we would call "frum". So it really behooves us – the Torah Jews – to keep the truth of the Torah alive through studying it, and understanding it according to our Mesorah and never let ourselves be vulnerable to the tremendous power of ignorance that allowed false religions to arise and dominate.

THE DESIGN OF A SHUL, AND WHAT IS IT MEANT TO TEACH US?

Many years ago I was living in Gateshead and used to travel every week to Newcastle to teach non-religious Jewish children in a Sunday Cheder. One of the projects we did was to make a model Shul.

To teach about the shul structure, I was advised by Rabbi Falk zt"l of Gateshead, to learn the sefer *Michtav Sofer* by Rav Shimon Sofer zt"l (son of the Chasam Sofer zt"l). He wrote this sefer in response to the Reform movement, which was actively perverting the traditional shul layout. This traditional design had remained unchanged for over two thousand years across Yemen, Syria, Israel, North and South America, England, Europe, and Morocco. I will share some of Rav Sofer's insights here.

We read in Yechezkel (11:16)

כן אמר כה־אמר אדני ה׳ כי הרחקתים בגוים וכי הפיצותים בארצות ואהי להם
למקדש מעט בארצות אשר־באו שם

Thus said the Hashem God I have indeed removed them far among the nations and have scattered them among the countries, and I have become to them a diminished sanctity in the countries whither they have gone.

Our Sages tell us that the words למקדש מעט (diminished sanctity) refers to the shul which resembles the בית המקדש. Each of the traditional features of the shul symbolises a part of the בית המקדש.

ארון קודש Aron Kodesh 'holy chest'

The ארון קודש (called the heichal—היכל by Sephardic Jews) resembles the Aron Ha'Edus (The Aron of the testimony). The Luchos were inside the ארון קודש, today it houses the sifrei Torah. The ארון קודש in a shul is almost always positioned in such a way such that those who face it are facing towards Jerusalem.

עמוד Omud

The Shliach Tzibur davens before the עמוד. It resembles the Mizbeach Ha'Ketores, the incense altar which stood inside the Heichal in front of the Kodesh Kedoshim. Likewise, tefilla is called avodah she'b'lev, since it resides inside a person's heart. Tefilla should be a joyous experience. The service of incense makes a person happy as it says in Proverbs (27:9): שמן וקטרת ישמח־לב *oil and incense gladden the heart...* the original aromatherapy!

בימה Bimah

The bimah recalls the Mizbeach Ha'Nechoshes (the copper altar) where sacrifices were offered. The bimah is situated in the center of the shul in order that everyone can hear the reading of the Torah. The Torah reading replaces communal sacrifices offered in the בית המקדש. If they took place at the side of the shul, not everyone would be able to hear the Torah reading. It would be as if a Jew does not have a chelek (portion) in the sacrifices.

I was recently davening in "basement shteeble", where I was surprised to see the bimah placed to the side of the room, due to space constraints. However, I noticed that Rabbi Yehoshua Pfeffer cites a teshuvah from Rav Moshe Feinstein zt"l (Iggros Moshe Orach Chaim II, no. 41) to the effect that, because this is only a question of custom, there is no need to be stringent and squeeze the bimah into the center of a shul. Rav Moshe adds (no. 42) that it is permitted (when the need arises) to pray in a shul whose בימה is not centered. Although the Chasam Sofer staunchly opposed moving the bimah, this opposition was meant for his generation due to the battle against Reform.)

נר תמיד Ner Tomid

The "eternal light" hangs from the ceiling of the shul just in front of the ארון. It resembles the Ner Maaravi of the Menorah which burned continuously in the Heichal in front of the Aron Ha' Edus. During Chanukah we place the Menorah in the Shul on the southside just as the Menorah was placed in the heichal on the south side of the בית המקדש. It is interesting to note that many lights are lit in a shul to show respect and honor to its sanctity, as it says in Yeshayahu (24:15) עַל־כֵּן בָּאֻרִים כַּבְּדוּ ה' : therefore, honor Hashem with lights.

Peroches

Aryeh Citron writes that preferably, the peroches (curtain) should hang outside the door of the ארון. It resembles the curtain that shielded the ארון קודש that was in the בית המקדש. (*Shemos* 26:33). (Shaarei Halacha U'Minhag, vol. 1, p. 198. See Responsa Yechaveh Daas (6:9). See also Talmud, Megillah 26b; Rashi ibid., s.v. Perisah; and Tosafos ibid., s.v. MeReish.)

Magen Dovid (מגן, lit. Shield)

The six-pointed star is sometimes found on the peroches. It is called Magen Dovid because Dovid Hamelech had complete trust in Hashem who is the king both above and below and four corners of the world. Therefore he did not fear the gentile nations with whom he waged War (See Iggeres Moshe part 3 para 15).

Windows

The Gemara in Brachos 34b states:

אמר רבי חייא בר אבא אמר רבי יוחנן: אל יתפלל אדם אלא בבית שיש שם חלונות.
שנאמר: "וכוין פתיחן ליה בעליתה (לקבל) [נגד] ירושלם"

Rabbi Ḥiyya bar Abba said that Rabbi Yoḥanan said: One may only
pray in a house with windows, as then he can see the heavens and
focus his heart, as it is stated with regard to Daniel's prayer: "In his
attic, there were open windows facing Jerusalem" (Daniel 6:11).

Ideally, shuls should have 12 windows in the sanctuary, although
not all of them must face Jerusalem. Some interpret this number to
correspond with the 12 tribes.

The Height of the shul

The Gemara Shabbos 11a states that any city whose roofs are higher than the shul will ultimately be destroyed because of the contempt
shown the shul. According to our halacha, the shul should be the tallest
building in the city. (*Orach Chaim* 151 Mishnah Berurah). In modern
cities, however, this is not practical. It is therefore permitted to build a
house taller than the shul—though preferable to avoid doing so wherever possible.

Our great Sages designed the shul in such a way that, wherever we
live during this long exile, we will be reminded of the בית המקדש. We
will feel shame that we have forfeited this precious gift as a result of our
sins. This, in turn, will awaken our desire for Hashem to rebuild the בית
המקדש and our tefillos will be thus inspired.

The link between our avodah she'b'lev and the Temple sacrifices
is further alluded to in the Korbanos section of Shacharis. There, the
word עונותינו is used in two separate locations both describing how the
בית המקדש was destroyed because of our sins. Maybe one can say that
the double reference of עונותינו may refer to the destructions of first and
the second בית המקדש.

Yechezkel's prophecy regarding the למקדש מעט (diminished sanctity) cited above continues with Hashem's promise that eventually we
will be gathered in from our scattered locations across the globe and

brought back to Eretz Yisroel (*Yechezkel* 11:16-20). We need not despair of redemption. In the meantime, we can remember that Shul is not just about a place to "chap a minyan". Its very structure connects us to the Beis HaMikdash of old. Through focussing our tefillos this way, we hope we will merit to see it rebuilt speedily and in our days.

יהי רצון מלפניך ה׳ אלקינו ואלקי אבותינו שיבנה בית המקדש במהרה בימינו ותן חלקנו בתורתך: ושם נעבדך ביראה כימי עולם וכשנים קדמוניות

May it be Your will, Hashem our God and God of our fathers, that the Holy Temple be rebuilt speedily in our days: and grant us our share in Your בית *Torah. And there we will serve You reverently as in the days of old and in earlier years.*

A FAREWELL SPEECH

everal of our married children have settled in Lakewood, New Jersey, and my wife and I decided recently it was time to move to the United States to be near them. When I shared the news with my friends in Montreal, particularly those in my shul, they were saddened but fully understood our decision.

After coming to Montreal from England for my Jewish educational program over 20 years ago, this decision to leave was difficult. Living in Montreal produced many memorable moments including being able to publish my book, "I CAN Learn" (Feldheim) and prepping my next book about my Rebbe, HaRav HaGaon Rabbi Mattisyahu Salomon, called "A Talmid's Journey", which I hope to see in the Jewish book-stores before Yomtov.

In the weeks leading up to our move, I was deeply touched by our shul Rav, who organised a *seudas preida* on Shabbos and I had the honor of addressing the kehillah just before Mussaf.

Since it was just after Shavuos, I drew inspiration from Midrash Rus, which I had recently studied.

In Sefer Rus, we read about Rus and Orpah:

ותשאנה קולן ותבכינה עוד ותשק ערפה לחמותה ורות דבקה בה

And they raised their voices and wept again, and Orpah kissed her mother-in-law, but Rus cleaved to her" (Rus 1:14).

The Midrash offers a fascinating insight into this scene:

ותשק ערפה לחמותה, כל נשיקה של תפלות בר מן תלת, נשיקה של גדלה, ונשיקה
של פרקים, ונשיקה של פרישות

*"Orpah kissed her mother-in-law" All kisses are of licentiousness,
except for three: a kiss of greatness, a kiss of absence, and a kiss of
parting (Rus Rabbah 2:21).*

The Etz Yosef writes:

בר מן תלת

ועניין הנשיקה היא התדבקות רוחא ברוחא. ועל כן כאשר נתמנה אדם לגדולה
שאינו ראוי לה צריך נשיקות הנביא. להאציל ולתן עליו מרוחו ויצלח למלוכה כמו
שאול שהמלוכה היה שאול לו שהמלוכה שייך לבית דוד כדתיב לא יסור שבט
מיהודה לכן נשקו שמואל. אבל לדוד לא נשק בעת משחו אותו למלך משום שהיה
ראוי מצד השבט למלוכה. ומהטעם הזה בעצמו הנשיקה בהתחבר הרחוקים
והנפרדים לשוב להיות לאחדים ורוח אחד לכל. ועל זה הדרך הנפרדים איש מעל
אחיו ינשקו זה את זה לחבר הרוח הנתק. על דרך אומרם ז"ל הנפטר מחברו אל
יפטור אלא מתוך דבר הלכה שמתוך כך זכרו. והוא מבואר (אגרת שמואל)

A kiss represents the attachment of Ruach to Ruach. When someone
is appointed to a position for which they are not naturally suited, it is
necessary for the kisses of a novi to make him a nobleman and give from
his ruach that he will be successful in his kingship. This is akin to the
case of Shaul, whose kingship was borrowed, since the kingship rightly
belonged to the house of Dovid, as it is written לא־יסור שבט מיהודה *"The
scepter shall not depart from Yehudah"* (*Bereshis* 49:10) Thus, Shmuel
kissed him. However, Dovid was not kissed at the time of his anointing as
king, because he was inherently worthy of kingship by virtue of his tribe
Yehuda and for this reason, a kiss signifies the union of distant and separate entities, merging them into a single ruach. Therefore, those who are
parting from each other, kiss to reconnect the Ruach that is being pulled
away. This aligns with the saying of Chazal that one who is parting from
his friend should not do so except through a matter of halacha (*Brochos*
31a) so that through this, he will be remembered. (Iggeres Shmuel).

The Eliyahu Zuta writes whenever he recalls the one from whom he
took leave, he will think well of him because of the new halacha that he
taught him.

With a touch of humor, I added, "I am not going to kiss every-body here—that would be a problem, wouldn't it?" The congregation laughed. "I'll give you a bear hug instead".

I also told the shul members about my recent deviation from writing solely about Jewish education to now documenting current events as I feel compelled to address widespread misinformation. Even some Yidden I've spoken to, or who have emailed me regarding my articles have been unfortunately misled by the lies perpetuated by social media.

To stop Yidden from being misled by the left-wing media, I turn my attention to Chazal and publish what they say about current events, helping us understand the correct path to think and follow Hashem and see the hand of Hashem orchestrating everything in our lives.

For example, in a recent article entitled "The Verdict on Soon-to-be President Donald Trump" I discussed how the verdict against Donald Trump was based on total falsehoods, according to my understanding and interpretation of Chazal. The article was published in the Jewish Tribune on Wednesday, June 26. The following week, on Monday, July 1, the Supreme Court rejected the claims, aligning with my argument that the allegations were unfounded.

What We Can Learn from the Holocaust?

Over seventy years have passed since the Holocaust ended in 1945. Although we cannot understand Hashem's ways and have to accept that ultimately the churban was for our good, nevertheless we continue to ask: "What lessons can be learned from the Holocaust, and how can we transmit these lessons to future generations?"

When we look at the stories in Nach (especially at the Neviim Rishonim), we find that whenever Bnei Yisroel sinned, Hashem would bring an enemy to attack. The Jewish response would always be to cry out to Hashem, so that Hashem would bring them a yeshua. For example King Sancheriv besieged Yerushalayim with 185,000 thousand troops. King Chezkiah cried out to Hashem and made all the Yidden do teshuvah. The next morning they woke up to find all the invading troops had died.

They realised that the reason why Hashem brought the enemy to inflict harm was to wake them up to their duty to serve Hashem properly and follow the Torah's ways. In other words, the Yidden themselves had to change in order to prevent any more calamities from happening.

After the Churban the Jews said "Never Again". But did we change our ways sufficiently? Are we utilizing the lessons from Nach? We have just experienced another Tisha B'Av in mourning. Moshiach did not come. Jews face ongoing personal and national tragedies. In what area should we improve?

As a mechanech who helps many students struggling with their learning at all ages and stages I perceive one crucial element we are failing to transmit to the next generation of Yidden. It is simcha. What do I mean by this? In parshas Teruma (26:13), Rashi comments on the fact that the yerios draped down until they covered the silver adanim. Rashi quotes the Chazal, "the Torah is teaching us Derech Eretz, that a person should care for and protect (chas) that which is beautiful and precious." What could be more beautiful and precious than the pure neshamos our own children? Yet for lack of simcha in the classroom, children drop out of school and out of Yiddishkeit. Whenever a child gets thrown out of school there is a kitrug in shomayim.

What does this have to do with the Holocaust?

The year was 1941. A boy was sent from his small village to learn in yeshiva. Meanwhile, the Germans came and wiped out his family, leaving only a great aunt (a World War I veteran's widow) in the house. The boy's teacher tried to protect him from learning of this tragedy by forging letters from his parents. Eventually he realised that the letters weren't in his father's handwriting so he decided to go back home to see what was happening.

Upon arrival the great aunt broke the tragic news to him. She informed him that the Germans were coming back and that he must leave immediately. Just then the Gestapo pulled up, so he quickly ran into the forest where, after a day of walking, he reached the border with Hungary. There he went to the nearest kehilla. He had no family there, but he wanted to learn.

I wish I could tell you that the boy was warmly embraced by his fellow Jews and offered a comforting refuge for body and soul. In truth, as this story was relayed to me decades later by his now son-in-law, the boy went to the cheder but they told him that to be able to learn there, he would have to pay tuition. He told them "I have no money. I just lost my entire family". They told him it was too bad. All he had was his pocket money which he had stashed away and he gave it to them.

A young girl was sent to Auschwitz. The train arrived at night so she was able to pass the selection without anyone noticing how young she was. When it came to the next selection her mother suggested that she should get a mop and try to pretend to be a part of the cleaning crew to be able to pass through the cordon of S.S. soldiers. She did this and successfully passed the selection the second time. Finally they came to a block. I wish I could tell you that this young girl was warmly embraced by her fellow Jews, who, Recognising her young age rallied round to protect her. In truth, as this account was relayed to me, the girl was shunned for belonging to the wrong religious group. A young girl who had been miraculously spared from death by the Nazis several times could not escape the sinas chinam within her own people.

Just after the war, a family was living in Bnei Brak. The father had to go to Miluim (a yearly statutory army service for a few weeks). In those days soldiers had to serve for a few weeks a year without getting paid for that time. Unable to work during the army service, the father had no money to pay for school fees. I wish I could tell you that the school extended credit to the impoverished family not wanting to risk damage to the precious neshamos they had in their care. In truth, since the family couldn't pay, the children were sent home.

Years later when one of those children, now grown and married, was living in Canada, that same school approached him for a donation. He reminded them that they had thrown him out because of lack of money. He donated anyway.

Lack of achdus within the community, vulnerable children being sent away from yeshiva because they cannot pay. This was the situation around the time of the Holocaust. Almost 70 years later, can we honestly say these problems are things of the past?

I receive emails from parents all over the frum community sharing their painful stories of how their beautiful and precious children are treated in the school systems. A boy who ended up on drugs because he was a sensitive soul that got bullied and the school refused to intervene. A seventh grade rebbi who enlists the "bad middos kids" to be his henchmen to keep order in the classroom by hurting kids who get in his way. A sixth grade rebbi who slaps the kids. Kids who get thrown out of yeshiva for being too slow or too smart or too different.

It pains me to hear about all the suffering children. It pains me more that we haven't learned our lesson from the Holocaust in giving simcha and love of yiddishkeit to our children. I wish I could say these stories are outliers, and the vast majority of kids are happy and thriving, but the truth is, even one such story is one too many. Rabbi Avraham Twersky pointed out that the Missionaries spend hundreds of thousands of dollars to be able to convert just one Jew, whether in Israel or abroad. Yet we do not hesitate to throw a kid out of yeshiva.

Never again should a student be refused entry to a Jewish institution. Never again should a Jew feel rejected by his fellow Jews because he doesn't fit into the group. Never again should a student say "I hate Torah" because of their school experience.

I fully believe that once we have resolved to commit to this, it will be a tremendous zechus for us all and will bring Moshiach bimheirah b'yameinu.

THE OCTOBER 7 MASSACRE

הצור תמים פעלו כי כל־דרכיו משפט קל אמונה ואין עול צדיק וישר הוא

"The deeds of the [Mighty One] Rock are perfect, for all His ways are just; a faithful God, without injustice He is righteous and up-right." (Devarim 32:4)

Rashi explains: even though Hashem is strong [like a rock], when He brings retribution upon those who transgress His will, He does not bring it in a flood [of anger] but [rather] with justice because "His deeds are perfect."

תנא משמיה דרבי עקיבא: לעולם יהא אדם רגיל לומר: "כל דעביד רחמנא לטב עביד"

"It was taught in a baraysa in the name of Rabbi Akiva: One must always accustom oneself to say: 'Everything that God does, He does for the best.'" (Brachos 60b)

But sometimes things happen that are so horrible and unspeakable it is virtually impossible to see the goodness, the justice. In Israel October 7th the world witnessed a totally mind-boggling, terrible catastrophe where 1200 Jews were massacred in the most horrific manner. Hamas, an evil terrorist group, committed unspeakable acts violating married women then killing them, beheading babies, burning them in ovens, and destroying houses with people in them. The horrors pained every single Jew in the world, religious or not religious.

We are told that more Jews died on that one day than on any day since the holocaust. For many, it feels like a second Holocaust. To get a sense of the magnitude of this calamity, it has been said that what happened on October 7th is equivalent to 200 9/11's happening in one day.

Our lives will be changed forever by this.

Can one reconcile the above statements from the Torah and the Gemara about Hashem seeking retribution with kindness and justice, with the horrors of these events? Where can we see the kindness and goodness of Hashem? Of course, we cannot begin to know or understand the heavenly cheshbonos or the mysterious ways of Hashem, but by looking closely at the many stories that are emerging from that infamous day, we see a clear message about shmiras Shabbos.

Many kibbutzim and settlements were invaded by terrorists that day, but I heard, two settlements remained untouched. Hamas tried to enter, but the gates were shut *because it was Shabbos*. These Sabbath-observant moshavim were spared. A video security camera documented terrorists trying to enter a different moshav but being unable to get in. They waited patiently and a few minutes later a car with one of the inhabitants of the moshav drove up. Just as the gate opened, these evil animals came and killed him and then they went inside to wreak havoc and destruction. The whole settlement became a target.

The following Shabbos I was singing zemiros with my family. I don't always pay attention to the words, since they are so familiar. This time I happened to put my mind to it and was struck by the powerful message of the zemer.

כי אשמרה שבת קל ישמרני, אות היא לעולמי עד בינו וביני

If I safeguard the Shabbos, Hashem will safeguard me. It is a sign forever and ever between Him and me.

This zemer was written close to a thousand years ago by Abraham ben Meir Ibn Ezra (1092-1167) and is sung in Jewish homes the world over at the Shabbos table. The message is clear and became even clearer in the aftermath of the recent massacre. Keeping Shabbos protects us.

It is a sign. Just as the angel of death knew to pass over the homes in Mitzrayim that had blood painted on the doorpost, our keeping Shabbos is a sign between Hashem and His people that indicates that we are deserving of special protection.

In the last paragraph, we sing:

מחל מלאכה בו סופו להכרית for doing desecrating work on it (Shabbos) his end will be excision.

Those two Moshavim were saved because they kept Shabbos. The non-shomer Shabbos moshavim was unfortunately not spared. We cannot understand Hashem's cheshbon as to when He decides a person has finished his tafkid in the world, but this should be a siman to us and to all Jews. Hashem loves us and he gave us Shabbos as a special gift only for Klal Yisroel. Keeping His gift safe protects us.

Similar stories have been pouring in, such as this account from a secular woman:

> I took knives and went into the bomb shelter. I gave each of my children two knives and said to them "Listen up this is not a normal situation, it's a situation that has never happened". Suddenly I looked through the keyhole of the door and saw six terrorists with drawn guns chanting in Arabic. In that terrifying moment, I looked up to Hashem and cried out "I promise you one thing that I'll keep every Shabbos until the day I die!" At that moment I looked again and they had vanished.

Another story heard from Rabbi Yosef Mizrachi and widely publicised on Israeli radio describes how Rabbi Mizrachi made a Shabbaton in Eretz Yisroel this past Elul. Two secular girls were so inspired they committed to keeping Shabbos from then on. They went to the music festival on Friday, October 6th. As it was coming close to Shabbos, they decided to leave. They took three more girls with them. The terrorists came in soon afterward. The girls were saved because they kept the Shabbos.

It has been over 70 years since the Nazis set up concentration camps across Europe for the purpose of systematically exterminating the Jews.

74

I heard on a recording from Rabbi Avigdor Miller that the very same boats used by Jews to profane the Shabbos in Germany before the war took them to the gas chambers during the war. There was tremendous assimilation and Shabbos desecration in the years preceding the holocaust, the extent of which was unprecedented in Jewish history.

Since the end of the Second World War, our rallying cry has been "Never Again". But it is still happening. We are still being slaughtered. What occurred on October 7th WAS another Holocaust. Bibi and his Commanders keep saying "We must destroy Hamas so that this won't happen again", but it is unlikely that this tactic will succeed. Hamas leaders repeatedly state that bombs will not prevent them from continuing their "holy mission" to eradicate the Jewish people chas v"shalom.

So is there anything we can do to prevent such things from happening again? The answer will not have anything to do with armies, peace treaties, or cease-fires. In my previous article, I stated that I was not a novi, only relaying what chazal has told us, and this will provide a glimpse of what we can do to prevent it from happening again.

The answer to "never again" is given by Moshe Rabbeinu in the Torah (*Devarim* 30:16) reassuring us that if you keep the Torah, the Commandments, (including holy Shabbos), "you will live in security and peace in our land."

There is always more we can do to strengthen our commitment to Torah and mitzvos. So long as there are Jews among us not keeping Shabbos, we know there is more work to do. As Rabbi Yisroel Salanter was reputed to have said:

> *"If someone talks loshon horo in the beis midrash in Kovno, Jews will desecrate the Shabbos in Paris."*

All of Klal Yisroel is responsible for one another and our actions can make a difference to the spiritual choices of even our secular brothers and sisters. "Never again" depends on the Jews keeping the Shabbos. Hashem is giving us a wake-up call to strengthen ourselves in Torah and Mitzvos and especially Shabbos as a shmira for Klal Yisroel.

I would like to finish off it with a gemara in *Yevamos 63a*

אמר רבי אלעזר בר אבינא: אין פורענות באה לעולם אלא בשביל ישראל, שנאמר:
"הכרתי גוים נשמו פנותם החרבתי חוצותם", וכתיב: "אמרתי אך תיראי אותי תקחי
מוסר"

*Rabbi Elazar bar Avina said: Calamity befalls the world only due
to the sins of the Jewish people, as it is stated: "I have cut off nations,
their corners are desolate; I made their streets waste" (Tzefaniah
3:6), and it is written: "I said: Surely you will fear Me, and take
chastisement" (Tzefaniah 3:7).*

All the more so when the calamity falls upon us directly like this
massacre on the 7th of October we should assume responsibility תקחי
מוסר, take chastisement, fear Hashem, and heed to His word in all its
details and follow the Torah.Then we will have complete security in
our Eretz Yisroel, as it is so clearly stated in our Torah. With this, may
we merit to be able to greet Moshiach in our lifetime.

"A WAKE-UP CALL FROM HEAVEN: UNDERSTANDING THE CHALLENGES OF OUR TIMES THROUGH TORAH"

As many of you know, I spend my days teaching students from all walks of life, especially those who are reconnecting with their Jewish roots. This journey is incredibly rewarding, but it also comes with its challenges. I often find myself addressing complex questions that go beyond the lesson plan. These questions aren't just about Torah study; they are about making sense of the world around us through the lens of our faith.

Recently, one of my clients, a Baal Teshuva from California now studying in Israel, asked a question that struck a chord with me—and I believe it will resonate with many of you as well. This client, who has been immersed in intense study for six months, is grappling with the situation in Israel. He asked, "Why does it seem like evil is winning? Why are there still hundreds of thousands of Jews in shelters, unable to return home due to the threat from Arab terrorists? The rockets, the attacks, the antisemitism—why does it seem like we are always under siege? And why does the promise that we will be as numerous as the stars seem so far from reality?"

This is a question that I believe we all wrestle with, especially in times of crisis. Whether it's the seemingly endless conflicts in Israel, the political turmoil we see worldwide, or even the personal struggles we face in our daily lives, these challenges can sometimes make us question the promises we've held onto for so long.

And yet, I believe that these events, as troubling as they are, can be understood in a different light when viewed through the lens of our Torah. The Torah doesn't shy away from acknowledging the hardships that the Jewish people will face. but we have a promise Hashem made to Avraham—that his descendants would be as numerous as the stars—is indeed true.

This is not a contradiction; it is a profound truth about our relationship with Hashem. As the Midrash Rabbah teaches in *Shemot Rabbah* (*1:16*), וירב העם, לקים מה שנאמר מי זה אמר ותהי ה' לא צוה (איכה ג, לז) אם פרעה. צוה להרג את הזכרים מה הועיל בגזרתו ה' לא צוה — "The people increased," to fulfill what is stated: "Who has commanded and it came to pass, unless Hashem ordained it?" (*Eichah* 3:37). No decree can take effect unless Hashem commands it. Even when evil seems triumphant, we must remember that everything is ultimately under Hashem's control. Pharaoh's decree to kill all the male children of Israel was nullified because it wasn't aligned with Hashem's will.

But the evil today is getting worse and worse. The Midrash implies that such events must be decreed by Hashem. Tragically, even the horrors of October 7th, when we experienced what many are calling a genocide, could only have happened because Hashem decreed it.

Here's where I want to touch on a crucial point that my client raised: Why does this evil keep happening to the Jewish people, not just now, but for thousands of years? The answer, I believe, lies in the very words of Moshe Rabbeinu. Before his death, Moshe predicted that the Jewish people would rebel against Hashem and suffer as a result. In *Devarim* (*31:29*), he said, "כי ידעתי, אחרי מותי כי-השחת תשחתון, וסרתם מן-הדרך אשר צויתי אתכם; וקראת אתכם הרעה, באחרית הימים, כי תעשו את-הרע, בעיני ה', להכעיסו, במעשה ידיכם" — "For I know that after my death you will surely become corrupt and turn from the way I have commanded you. In days

78

to come, disaster will fall on you because you will do evil in the sight of Hashem and arouse His anger by what your hands have made."

October 7th is no exception to this. It was meant to be the happiest time of the year, the completion of Torah, *Simchas Torah*. It's a wake-up call to all of us, religious and non-religious alike, that we must love each other and help bring each other closer to Hashem and His Torah. As Moshe told the Yidden,. As it says in *Devarim (30:1-3)*,

והיה כי יבאו עליך כל - הדברים האלה הברכה והקללה אשר נתתי לפניך והשבת
אל - לבבך, בכל הגויים, אשר הדיחך ה' אלקיך שמה ושבת - עד ה' אלקיך ושמעת
בקולו ככל אשר אנכי מצוך היום אתה ובניך בכל לבבך ובכל נפשך ושב ה' אלקיך
את שבותך ורחמך ושב וקבצך מכל העמים אשר הפיצך ה' אלקיך שמה

"When all these blessings and curses I have set before you come on you and you take them to heart wherever Hashem your God disperses you among the nations, and when you and your children return to Hashem your God and obey Him with all your heart and with all your soul according to everything I command you today, then the Lord your God will restore your fortunes and have compassion on you and gather you again from all the nations where He scattered you."

The message is clear: the suffering we have endured for centuries is solely because we have not followed Hashem's way- we sinned against Him.

Our history is filled with moments where the Jewish people have faced tremendous adversity. But each time, these challenges have served as a catalyst for introspection and spiritual renewal. This pattern is evident throughout the Tanach, where moments of crisis are followed by repentance and eventual redemption.

In the Haftarah for Shabbos Shuva, the Prophet Hoshea calls out to the Yidden, urging them to return to Hashem with the words: "שובה ישראל עד ה' אלקיך, כי כשלת בעונך"—"Return, Israel, to Hashem your God. Your sins have been your downfall" (*Hoshea 14:2*). This message is clear: our hardships are not meaningless; they are a direct result of our actions and a call to return to our roots. embrace our role as "a light unto the nations," we can alter the course of our destiny.

The Torah is not just a historical document; it is a living guide that holds the solutions to our modern-day challenges. If we return to its teachings and In this context, antisemitism, as painful as it is, can be seen as a Divine nudge, pushing us to return to our true purpose. The difficulties we face, whether from external threats or internal divisions, are all opportunities to strengthen our connection to Hashem and to one another. As the siddur says, "ומפני חטאינו גלינו מארצנו"— "And due to our sins, we were exiled from our land." (Shalosh Regalim Mussaf)

This is not just a statement of historical fact; it is a reminder of the cause-and-effect relationship between our actions and our circumstances.

So, what can we do? We must start by looking inward, examining our own lives and our communities. Are we truly living up to the standards set by the Torah? Are we treating each other with the respect and love that is required of us? Are we doing our part to bring the light of the Torah to the world?

This is not a message of despair but of hope. The Torah assures us that we return to Hashem,. As it says in *Devarim* (30:4), "אם־יהיה נדחך בקצה השמים, משם יקבצך ה' אלקיך, ומשם יקחך"— "Even if you have been banished to the most distant land under the heavens, from there Hashem your God will gather you and bring you back."

This promise is as relevant today as it was thousands of years ago. Our return to Hashem will bring about our redemption, both individually and as a nation. In closing, I urge all of us to take this time to reflect on our lives and our actions. Let us use this period of turmoil to strengthen our commitment to the Torah and mitzvos, to increase our acts of kindness, and to reach out to all those who need chizuk. Together, we can bring about the ultimate redemption, the coming of Mashiach, and the fulfillment of the promise that we will be as numerous as the stars in the sky.

May we all merit to see that day soon.

Reflections on Iran's Threats Through the Lens of the Midrash Rabbah (Esther)

In the tumultuous weeks leading up to Pesach, amidst the backdrop of escalating tensions between Iran and Israel, I found myself seeking solace and guidance in the timeless wisdom of Chazal. In particular, I turned to the teachings of Midrash Esther, drawn to its narrative of resilience and triumph in the face of adversity. The story of Esther, with its central antagonist, Haman, who sought the destruction of Klal Yisroel, resonated deeply with the current events unfolding in the Middle East. Iran's threats against Israel echoed Haman's sinister plot, reminding us of the enduring struggle for survival and the resilience of our people throughout history.

As I delved into Midrash Esther, I discovered insights that spoke directly to our present-day situation. The parallels were striking: just as Esther and Mordechai confronted the threat posed by Haman, so too are we confronted with Iran's hostility.

Yet, amidst the uncertainty and fear, the teachings of Chazal offer a beacon of hope. The Midrash reminded me that despite the gravity of the situation, we are not alone. Just as Esther found courage and rallied her people to action, so too can we draw strength from our yerushah and unite in solidarity against the forces that seek to do us harm.

I shared these reflections with my neighbor one Shabbos morning, knowing that he, too, felt the weight of the world's troubles. As I recounted the chochmah of the Midrash, I could see the worry in his eyes begin to fade. "Don't be worried," I reassured him, echoing the timeless message of our Mesorah. "Just as our ancestors triumphed over adversity, so too will we overcome." I then showed my neighbor this amazing Midrash Esther (7:10).

Rabbi Shimon ben Yosei ben Lakonya's moshol between the Jewish people and rocks, and the nations of the world to pottery, is a profound reflection on the enduring strength and resilience of Klal Yisroel throughout history. The moshol draws from various posukim to illustrate the solidity and steadfastness of the Jewish nation.

By likening Bnei Israel to rocks and stones, Rabbi Shimon emphasises the enduring nature of Klal Yisroel, who has weathered countless trials and tribulations. Despite facing persecution and attempts at annihilation, we have remained steadfast and resilient, like rocks that withstand the test of time.

Conversely, the nations of the world are compared to pottery, which is fragile and easily broken. This analogy highlights the vulnerability of those who seek to harm or oppress us. Just as a clay pot would shatter when confronted with a rock, those who oppose Klal Yisroel will ultimately face their own downfall.

The reference to Nebuchadnezzar's dream from the sefer of Daniel further reinforces this message. The stone hewn from the mountain, symbolizing the Klal Yisroel ultimately triumphs over the iron, bronze, and clay, representing the powerful empires of the world. This prophetic imagery underscores the ultimate victory of the Klal Yisroel over their adversaries.

Rabbi Shimon's teachings convey a powerful message of hope, resilience, and the ultimate triumph of good over evil. It serves as a reminder of the enduring strength of the Jewish people and the futility of those who seek to harm them.

After discussing this Midrash with my neighbor, that Motzei Shabbos, Iran launched a massive attack against Israel, deploying approximately 170 drones, over 30 cruise missiles, and more than 120 ballistic missiles. Despite the overwhelming scale of the attack, Israel reported that Chasdei Hashem, 99 percent of the projectiles were successfully intercepted and neutralised.

The world, including many Jewish communities, understandably feared the potential devastation such an assault could bring upon Israel. The media, often leaning left, painted a grim picture of the situation, exacerbating concerns about the safety of the Jewish people.

Iran's explicit threat to punish Israel for its diplomatic presence in Syria only added to the tension. However, in a remarkable turn of events, Boruch Hashem, no Jewish lives were lost in the attack, save for one unfortunate incident where a 7-year-old bedouin girl was critically injured. This incident ironically served to diminish Iran's intended impact, making it a laughingstock in the eyes of many.

The outcome of the attack, where virtually all missiles were thwarted, was nothing short of a neis. It reminds us of the makkos that befell Paro and the mitzrim. Despite this undeniable display of Hashgacha Pratis, the response from the international community was muted. While some nations provided assistance, there was no widespread recognition of the miraculous nature of Israel's survival.

In retrospect, the events of that night should have prompted a greater acknowledgment of Divine Intervention and a rush towards embracing the faith of the Jewish people. Yet, the world remained largely indifferent, failing to grasp the significance of what had transpired. Nevertheless, the resilience of Klal Israel and the protection afforded to its people serves as a testament to the enduring strength and divine providence that has safeguarded the Jewish nation throughout history.

Historical examples, such as the downfall of Haman and various adversaries throughout Jewish history, serve as reminders of this principle. Similarly, the prophecy of Gog Umagog, in which hostile forces gather against Israel, ultimately culminates in their defeat.

Eitz Yosef writes in the above Midrash that when Gog Umagog will confront Israel in the future, they will meet a similar fate. Klal Yisroel, under the protection of Hashem, will emerge victorious, and their enemies will be vanquished.

Let us not forget the words we just recited at the Pesach Seder night: "והיא שעמדה" (And it has stood). This statement, originating from Chazal and embedded in the Haggadah, reflects our enduring mesorah. The Haggadah was compiled during the Mishnaic and Talmudic periods, although its exact date remains unknown. Despite this uncertainty, this statement has persisted throughout history for over 1500 years.

"And it has stood" symbolises the resilience that has defined our people across generations. We have faced numerous trials throughout history, from the destruction of the two Batei HaMikdash, the Spanish Inquisition, the Crusades, pogroms in Europe, the blood libels, the horrors of the Nazis, and ongoing conflicts such as the Arab-Israeli wars since 1948. The most recent atrocities, like the October 7th Massacre, serve as painful reminders of the threats we continue to confront.

Today, chants for our destruction echo worldwide, from campus demonstrations to street protests. The voices of those who seek our annihilation resound, declaring their intent to eradicate us "from the land to the sea" and cast us into oblivion. Yet, in the face of these challenges, we find solace in the concluding words of "והיא שעמדה" "**And the Blessed Holy One saves us from their hands.**"

The Abudarham from the 14th century writes something remarkable -that In every generation Hashem arranges that someone should arise who will want to harm us, and He does so that He will be able to save us from them. **This demonstrates to the whole world that we are Hashem's special people and that He watches over us.** (The Me'am Lo'ez haggadah)

84

FROM HAMAN TO HAMAS: REFLECTIONS ON WEALTH, POWER, AND DIVINE JUSTICE

It has long been a source of curiosity how historical figures like Korach and Haman the Agagite acquired wealth. Korach, known from the Chumash, and Haman, from the Book of Esther, rose to prominence without apparent business ventures to explain their riches.

In the case of Korach, his wealth remains a mystery, especially during his time in Mitzrayim. No recorded business endeavors or investments could account for his immense fortune. Haman, once in extreme poverty, sold himself as a slave to Mordechai. (*Yalkut Shimoni Nach* (1056:18),referenced by Rashi in explaining *Megillah* 15a).

It also states in the Gemara (*Megillah* 16a) תנא: המן, ספר של כפר קרצום היה עשרים ושתים שנה

> *We are taught in a baraisa: Haman was the barber of the village of Kartzum for twenty-two years.*

Due to this, Haman's sudden emergence as a billionaire raises questions. His success was due to what?

This scenario parallels a contemporary issue—the wealth of the top leaders of Hamas. Reports suggest that these leaders are collectively worth billions of dollars. However, the origins of their wealth are unclear. How did these people earn this money? Through legitimate means, akin to President Trump's real estate ventures? Or did their wealth come from less transparent sources?

Calls for transparency, such as the release of tax returns, echo the scrutiny faced by public figures like Trump. Democrats, for instance, have demanded access to Trump's financial records for accountability. Yet, similar demands regarding the wealth of Hamas leaders seem absent. It's essential to question the accountability of individuals with significant wealth, regardless of their affiliations. Transparency measures, including financial disclosures, are crucial for maintaining public trust and ensuring that wealth accumulation is ethical and lawful.

The Midrash Esther (7:5) answers the question of how figures like Korach and Haman accumulated wealth.

Rabbi Pinchas said two wealthy men emerged in history, one from Israel and one from the idolatrous nations, both ultimately leading to their downfall.

In the case of Korach, his wealth was acquired through discovering the treasures of gold and silver concealed by Yosef and he stole it for himself. Haman amassed his wealth by seizing the treasures of the kings of Yehudah and also stealing them for himself.

The same parallel with Hamas leaders: the US and EU taxpayers think that they pay for supplies for their people, and the best example is agricultural supplies.

The leaders snatch water pipes they buy with European and American money and send them to workshops where these pipes turn into rocket fuselages. They **steal** fertilisers and other chemicals that are sent to help promote local agriculture and send those to labs that turn them into rocket propellants and warhead explosives.

The IDF found an amass of stolen money in Gaza ready to be used to perpetuate their bomb-making plans.

So why did Hashem make these evil Hamas leaders wealthy?

The Midrash Esther (7:2) provides the answers and Rabbi Levi expounds on the posuk:

בפרח רשעים כמו עשב ויציצו כל פעלי און, מה כתיב בסוף קרייה: להשמדם עדי עד

When the wicked bloom like grass, and all evildoers flourish (*Tehillim* 92:8) ; and completes the posuk: *It is to destroy them till eternity.*

Haman was made great only to his detriment, so why did Hashem make him great?

The same Midrash continues to say that the reason for his greatness is analogous to a common soldier who cursed the king's son. The king said: If I kill him, everyone will say: He killed a common soldier. (No one would pay attention to him) He appointed him to be an officer, and afterward, a commander, and then beheaded him. So Hashem said: Had Haman been killed when he went down and advised Achashverosh to cancel the construction of the Beis HaMikdash, no one would have known him. Rather, let him be made great and then be hanged. Eitz Yosef quoting Menos Halevi says "For then his punishment would cause a greater sanctification of Hashem's name." The Midrash continues "he set his seat above all the princes who were with him," and then, "they hanged Haman." The enemies of Hashem are made great for their downfall, and it is written משגיא לגוים ויאבדם: "He exalts the nations and eliminates them" (*Iyov* 12:23).

We can now fully understand what is happening with the Hamas leaders. But what will happen to all the money the leaders have stolen? The Midrash *Bamidbar Rabba* (22:7) answers this question.

כן ירמיה אומר (ירמיה ט, כב כג): כה אמר ה' אל יתהלל חכם בחכמתו ואל יתהלל הגבור בגבורתו אל יתהלל עשיר בעשרו, כי אם בזאת יתהלל וגו', ומתנות אלו בזמן שאינן באין מן הקדוש ברוך הוא סופן להפסק ממנו

Yermiyahu states (9:22)

"*Thus says Hashem, "Let not the wise boast in their wisdom, nor the strong boast in their strength, nor the wealthy boast in their wealth. So these gifts, when they do not come from Hashem, they will finally be cut off from them*".

The Midrash continues with examples. Two wealthy men arose in the world, Korach from Israel and Haman from the nations of the world; but both of them were lost from the world. Why? Because their gift was not from Hashem but rather they grabbed it up for themselves.

The same is true with the leaders of Hamas who have grabbed the money and have taken it for themself. According to the Midrash, the consequence will be the same: they will finally be cut off from them. As the entire world can see in Gaza and now in Rafa, the IDF has discovered many tunnels costing billions of dollars which were built with stolen money, and "these gifts" will eventually be cut off from them.

Prime Minister Benjamin Netanyahu has stated clearly from the onset of the war on the 7th of October that complete victory is when Hamas will be eliminated.

As we know, Korach went on to die by the ground opening up and swallowing him. Haman was hanged. The Midrash states clearly why they were killed.

Midrash Bamidbar Rabbah (22:7).

ושניהם נאבדו מן העולם, למה, שלא היה מתנתן מן הקדוש ברוך הוא אלא חוטפין אותה להם

*they both perished from the world because the gifts did not come from Hashem but one who **grabs** these gifts for themselves.*

We can see this is exactly what is happening to the leaders and the terrorists of Hamas as they are slowly getting eliminated the same happened to Ebrahim Raisi, the former president of Iran and Second-in-Command, often referred to as the "Butcher of Tehran," who was killed this week in a helicopter crash.

In every generation, the Jewish people have faced adversaries seeking their destruction, echoing the timeless struggle against oppression and persecution.

Let us not forget what Moshe Rabbeinu said to Bnei Yisroel in *Devarim* (4:30)

בצר לך ומצאוך כל הדברים האלה באחרית הימים ושבת עד־ה׳ אלקיך ושמעת בקלו

*When you are **distressed**, and all these things happen upon you at*

88

the end of days, then you will return to the Lord your God and obey Him.

In the last 100 years, we have witnessed pogroms, Hitler YM"SH, Iran, Hamas, and now a tremendous upsurge in antisemitism found in universities around the world and on our streets. President Biden has shown his true colors by holding back arms to Israel to fight Hamas. He has given the green light for Hamas and anti-semitism to spread unabashedly in America and around the world.

As we confront the threats posed by entities like Hamas and Iran, it is natural to feel **distressed** and overwhelmed by the challenges we face. Yet, embedded within this **distress** is the call to return to Hashem, as the Torah writes clearly that we have received a promise from Hashem that we will all return. May our collective prayers and actions bring about the fulfillment of our hopes for peace, security, and the ultimate redemption of Mashiach and the building of the third Beis HaMikdash bimheira v'yameinu 'speedily and in our days' Amen.

HASHEM WILL NEVER FORSAKE US

Scary things are happening in the world. We face the reality that Israel may be on the brink of destruction from two fronts, chas v'shalom. From the outside, we fear Iran, who may have nuclear weapons very soon. They openly say they wish to destroy Israel, a country that comprises over 6 million Jews.

From the inside, the defeat of the left wing parties has caused tremendous political upheaval, demonstrations and protests. What do they really want? They want Israel to be a completely non-religious country. They want to live like Gentiles, satisfying their desires, doing as they please without rules or limitations from Hashem. The sad fact that Tel Aviv has become the "Gay center" of the world shows us where this is headed. If the High Court wins, we will no longer have a Jewish state. In a nutshell, the secular Jews are looking to nullify the Covenant that Hashem made with Avraham, making us the chosen people and a light to the world.

Is Hashen forsaking us??

Last Shabbos I found a beautiful midrash that was a source of comfort.

מדרש רבה אסתר פתיחתא סימן ד

שמואל פתח: (ויקרא כו, מד) : "ואף גם זאת בהיותם בארץ איביהם לא מאסתים

90

ולא גַעַלְתִּים לְכַלֹּתָם לְהָפֵר בְּרִיתִי אִתָּם כִּי אֲנִי ה' אֱלֹקֵיהֶם" "לֹא מְאַסְתִּים" - בְּבָבֶל,

"וְלֹא גַעַלְתִּים" - בְּמָדַי, "לְכַלֹּתָם", "לְהָפֵר בְּרִיתִי אִתָּם" -...

Shmuel opened his lecture on Megillas Esther quoting Parshas Be-
chukosai (Vayikra 26:44). After listing the punishments for dis-
obeying Hashem, the Torah ends with comfort. "When they are in
the land of their enemies, I will not reject them or abhor them so as
to destroy them completely, breaking my covenant with them. I am
the LORD their God.". The Midrash states that these four words:
"גַעַלְתִּים","לְכַלֹּתָם","לְהָפֵר" and "מְאַסְתִּים",each refer to one of the four
exiles. "I will not reject them" refers to Babylon, "abhor them" refers
to the exile of Persia-Medea, "destroy them completely" refers to the
exile of Greece, and "breaking my covenant with them" is Rome.

Eitz Yosef explains further: because Hashem exiled us to Bavel
from Israel, it appears He rejected us. So Hashem says מְאַסְתִּים, "I will
not reject them" in Bavel. He established Daniel, Hananiah, Mishael
and Azriah, who found favour and kindness and were granted wisdom
over all the wise men in Babylon. Hashem performed open miracles
for them as proof that Hashem did not reject the Jews.

גַעַלְתִּים "I abhor" means despised, made lower. This refers to Persia-Medea as it states in Megillas Esther (3:8), Haman said to King
Achashverosh "there is a certain group scattered and spread among all
the nationalities in all the lands of your Empire... it's not worthwhile
for the king to tolerate them". Yet Hashem established Mordechai and
Esther to bring the Jews back from the brink of extinction, and regain
their respect.

The Greeks wanted to destroy our souls by abolishing Torah and
mitzvos and forcing assimilation. But Hashem said לְכַלֹּתָם I will not destroy. He established Shimon Hatzadddik, Matisyahu ben Yochanan
the Kohen Gadol and his sons who restored Torah and mitzvos to the
Jewish people.

Finally, the midrash talks of Rome, the modern day Western Society. This exile might give the impression that Hashem has nullified
His Covenant as it has lasted so long and seems to be without end.

However, throughout it, Hashem has given us Torah scholars and great tzaddikim in every generation. This is clear evidence that He remains with us forever.

Even if the Jewish people fall to their lowest point, Hashem will not abrogate His Covenant with us.

Rabbi Ezriel Tauber writes in his book "Days Are Coming" that the Torah (*Devarim* 30:1) says that at the end of days all Jews will be in the midst of the nations to which they were exiled. This may be understood not only literally but figuratively. The Jews will have tried every fad, every philosophy, every culture. They will have indulged in everything the other nations offered. They will have explored everything except what lies within their hearts. However, from that very self-alienation, they will return to their roots with greater determination. Rabbi Tauber quotes the Sforno on that posuk that eventually we will reflect and be struck by the sharp contrast between truth of Torah and falsehood of our surrounding cultures and that will make us perceive how distant and alienated we are from Hashem and His Torah. Of this final repentance, our Sages say שמגעת עד כסא הכבוד, it reaches the Throne of Glory.

This prophecy has already started. It will surely continue. But this doesn't mean that we should simply sit back and wait. We have to do our responsibility and show Hashem we really want to come back home.

On a recent trip to Eretz Yisroel, I noticed remarkable changes. I had not been to Israel for over 30 years and I found Yerushalyim to be unrecognizable with new buildings, roads and trams, and the height of Tel Aviv's skyscrapers were dizzying. The Kosel tunnel museums were remarkable and the views from the Aish HaTorah balcony were breath-taking. One thing hadn't changed: the huge schism between the religious and the non-religious Jews.

When I was studying in yeshiva in Eretz Yisroel in the 1980s, there were 180 missionary groups. Today, according to Rabbi Skobac, founder of Jews for Judaism, there are at least 300. Have we correspondingly doubled the number of organizations bringing Jews back to Torah?

There is Chabad at Ben Gurion airport doing their wonderful work of encouraging non-religious Jews to don tefillin as early as 5:30am. Breslover Chassidim showing their simchas Hashem by dancing outside on streets in Yerushalayim with the goal of doing Kiruv. There are the great Aish Hatorah and Ohr Somayach institutions who do phenomenal jobs. But I also observed this 30 years ago. Other than a few more Kiruv organizations trying to do outreach, I did not see inherent Kiruv on the streets by frum Yidden. I observed the 2 sectors living side by side, but separately, focusing inward to their own world. With the dire matzav Klal Yisroel is in currently, it is incumbent upon us to do more.

In the Pesach Haggadah we sing "Kol Dichfin", we invite all who are hungry to come and eat. Why is this part of the Haggadah in Aramaic whilst the rest is in Hebrew? Because that was the language spoken by the ordinary Jew. The Haggadah wants to teach us we should invite any Jew who is hungry to come eat with us, regardless of their background.

So too, if anyone is hungry for Torah, we must openly invite them into our houses and we will teach them! As Jews, we are responsible for each and every one of them regardless of their situation, and we have to make sure they are given the opportunity to delve into the beauty of Torah. We have to bring back those who have left the derech, and make sure our children stay on the derech.

When I was a bochur, I remember Rav Shach ztz"l closed his yeshiva during the elections in Israel. All the students had to go out to vote for his political party, for the purpose of saving Klal Yisroel. In a similar vein, I would like to suggest that all yeshivos in Israel should dedicate several days each year to travel throughout Israel, speaking to unaffiliated Jews and bringing them back, spreading the message, "We love you, we love the Torah, let us teach it to you. We are both the same side of one coin."

In Meah Shearim, I noticed little has changed in 30 years. The same signs are displayed on the building walls asking people to dress modestly. Imagine if instead, the signs read:

כל היהודים שרוצים ללמוד את התורה הקדושה, בואו נשמח ללמד אתכם

All Jews who want to learn the holy Torah, come, we will be happy to teach you.

Shavuos is around the corner, and this is the time when ALL klal Yisroel were united in receiving the Torah from Moshe Rabbeinu and no one was left out. Let us rekindle the spark of our fellow brethren, whether it be a neighbor, co-worker or any unaffiliated Jew you may find on the street, and show them that they are part of this nation Yisroel. Kol areivim zeh le zeh.

THE VERDICT ON PRESIDENT DONALD TRUMP: A JEWISH PERSPECTIVE

O n May 30, 2024, President Donald Trump was found guilty of 34 felonies by a jury in his "hush money" trial in New York, making history as the first time that a president has been convicted of a crime. The trial, perceived as biased due to the involvement of only Democratic judges, was criticised for its lack of impartiality. This blatant bias, coupled with the political atmosphere of the city, has turned the constitution and the principle of impartial justice into a total mockery. America is now a laughing stock of the world.

It signals a dangerous erosion of law and order in a civilised country, where political agendas overshadow the pursuit of truth. From a Jewish perspective, what can we learn from this unprecedented event and its consequences for those who engage in such evil conduct and flout the law?

I would venture to compare the conviction of President Donald Trump to the account of Sodom in the Chumash, alongside Rambam's interpretation of collective accountability, which provides profound insights into the nature of justice, societal responsibility, and the consequences of inaction in the face of immorality.

Let's explore these concepts in greater depth.

Corruption and Perversion of Justice

The gemara in *Sanhedrin* 109b presents Sodom as a society where justice was entirely perverted..ארבע דייני היו בסדום שקראי ושקרורai זייפי. ומצלי דינא

There were four judges in Sodom and they were named for their actions: **Shakrai,** *meaning liar,* **and Shakrurai,** *habitual liar,* **Zayfai,** *forger,* **and Matzlei Dina,** *perverter of justice.*

Together they illustrate a legal system that consistently undermined fairness and integrity. Their rulings punished victims instead of perpetrators, highlighting systemic corruption that eroded the foundations of their society.

The Gemara brings down several cases of how the judges of Sodom perverted the law. As an example: In a case of one who strikes the wife of another and causes her to miscarry, they would say to the woman's husband: "Give the woman to the one who struck her, so that she will be impregnated for you again."

This perversion of justice mirrors the Trump trial, where perceived biases and extended procedures suggest a potential undermining of fairness.

Arrogance Born of Prosperity

ת״ר אנשי סדום לא נתגאו אלא בשביל טובה שהשפיע להם הקב״ה ומה כתיב בהם (איוב כח, ה) ארץ ממנה יצא לחם ותחתיה נהפך כמו אש מקום ספיר אבניה ועפרות זהב לו נתיב לא ידעו עיט ולא שזפתו עין איה לא הדריכוהו בני שחץ לא עדה עליו שחל

The Sages taught (Sanhedrin 109b) The people of Sodom became haughty and sinned due only to the excessive goodness that the Holy One, Blessed be He, bestowed upon them. And what is written concerning them, indicating that goodness? "As for the earth, out of it comes bread, and underneath it is turned up as it were by fire. Its stones are the place of sapphires, and it has dust of gold. That path no bird of prey knows, neither has the falcon's eye seen it. The proud beasts have not trodden it, nor has the lion passed thereby" (Job 28:5–8). The reference is to the city of Sodom, which was later overturned, as it is stated thereafter: "He puts forth His hand upon the flinty rock; He overturns the mountains by the roots" (Job 28:9).

Sodom's citizens, blessed with extraordinary wealth, fell into extreme arrogance and moral decay. Their prosperity fostered a false sense of invulnerability and a blatant disregard for divine commandments and basic human decency. This narrative serves as a powerful warning regarding the tendency for wealth and power to breed ethical complacency.

Trump's opponents Similarly, the immense financial and political power behind the forces against Trump have contributed to an environment where ethical considerations were overshadowed by the pursuit of power and victory. The arrogance born of this power can lead to moral decay, as seen in the relentless pursuit of Trump's conviction.As Trump mentioned they have a lot of money and I don't know where it's coming from.

Punishment of Kindness

הויא ההיא ריבתא דהות דהות קא מפקא ריפתא לעניא בחצבא איגלאי מלתא שפיוה דובשא ואוקמוה על איגר שורא אתא זיבורי ואכלוה והיינו דכתיב (בראשית יח, כ) ויאמר ה' זעקת סדום ועמורה כי רבה ואמר רב יהודה אמר רב על עיסקי ריבה

Sanhedrin 109b brings down a story regarding a young woman who would take bread out to the poor people in a pitcher so the people of Sodom would not see it. The matter was revealed, and they smeared her with honey and positioned her on the wall of the city, and the hornets came and consumed her. And that is the meaning of that which is written: "And the Lord said: Because the cry of Sodom and Gomorrah is great [rabba]" (Bereshis 18:20). And Rav Yehuda says that Rav says: Rabba is an allusion to the matter of the young woman [riva] who was killed for her act of kindness. It is due to that sin that the fate of the people of Sodom was sealed.

This story of the young woman punished for her act of charity ex-

97

emplifies the moral bankruptcy of Sodom. Her execution for feeding the poor highlights a society that punished compassion and rewarded cruelty. This underscores the severe consequences for societies that suppress altruism and kindness, leading to their ultimate downfall.

In Trump's case, the trial's atmosphere and the harsh treatment he received, despite his previous position as president, can be seen as a lack of compassion and an overemphasis on punishment. The absence of any leniency or consideration for his past contributions suggests a society quick to condemn without room for understanding or forgiveness.He did no wrong.

Donald Trump Speaks to the Nation After Conviction

Following his conviction, Donald Trump addressed the nation, highlighting statements given by the court in total conjunction with the White House and the Department of Justice. He emphasised that the legal proceedings were influenced by President Biden and his associates. Trump also pointed out the unprecedented imposition of a gag order, stressing that it has never been done before, especially as he is leading heavily in the polls.

I would add that this Democrat-led court system against Donald Trump is perpetuating a biased narrative, reminiscent of the injustices described in the Chumash. This is exactly how the court system worked in Sodom, a one-way system of evil as elaborated in the Gemara in Sanhedrin 109b.

Complete Accountability

The destruction of Sodom illustrates the principle of collective accountability. Everyone in the city was held responsible for the pervasive immorality and injustice, emphasizing that a society that tolerates or engages in widespread wrongdoing is collectively culpable. The Rambam's interpretation further elucidates that inaction in the face of wrongdoing implicates the entire community no one in Sodon made a demonstration to condone these evil rulings from the courts and people. In contemporary terms, the Democrats and their supporters, who are perceived as rejoicing over Trump's downfall without critically assessing the fairness of the proceedings, will face a collective moral reckoning. The societal impact of their actions, totally fabricated and unjust, will lead to severe repercussions, just as Sodom faced complete destruction. All those who vote or condone their actions will be destructed.

Hashem killed the inhabitants of Sodom instead of putting them in prison, why was their punishment so severely?

The Rambam to answer this in his Mishneh Torah, Laws of Kings (9:14).

וכיצד מצווין הן על הדינין חייבין להושיב דיינין ושופטים בכל פלך ופלך לדון בשש מצות אלו ולהזהיר את העם ובן נח שעבר על אחת משבע מצות אלו יהרג בסיף ומפני זה נתחייבו כל בעלי שכם הריגה שהרי שכם גזל והם ראו וידעו ולא דנוהו

How must the Noahides fulfill the commandment to establish laws and courts? They are obligated to set up judges and magistrates in every major city to render judgment concerning these six mitzvos and to admonish the people regarding their observance.

A Noachide who transgresses these seven commands shall **be executed by decapitation**. For this reason, all the men of Shechem were obligated to die. Shechem was kidnapped. They observed and were aware of his deeds, but did not judge him.

The stories of Sodom and Shechem illustrated the severe consequences for transgressing the Noahide laws. In Shechem, the men inhabitants were executed for failing to bring Shechem to justice after he kidnapped Dinah. Similarly, in Sodom, the corruption of the court system led to their complete destruction. Both cases resulted in execution by decapitation as a punishment for their grave sins.

Applying this principle to current events, the Democrats who have perverted the law against President Trump, making a mockery of justice. They have transgressed the Noahide laws by corrupting the judicial process with **liars, habitual liars, forgers**, and **perverters of justice** exactly how Sodon judges ruled. According to the teachings of our great Sages, it comes out that all those who support or vote for such people will be made accountable and face severe consequences- **executed by decapitation.**

A lesson to be learned for All Mankind - Obey Hashem's Will.

AN OPEN MIRACLE BY HASHEM FOR THE WORLD TO SEE

The attempted assassination of President Donald Trump on July 13 during a campaign event in Pennsylvania was a moment that many saw as an open miracle. My son-in-law shared with me how, after this assassination attempt, President Trump emerged as a different person—more humbled and introspective. This transformation was evident in his first public address following the incident, on Thursday, July 18 night, at the Republican National Convention in Milwaukee, where he openly discussed feeling God's protection during the attack. President Trump stated that he felt no fear and believed that Divine Intervention was at play. And I quote, as he was down on the ground after the shot he said to the audience at the convention *"I felt very safe. I had God on my side and I felt that."* Later he stated, *"I stand with you by the grace of the Almighty God,"* and further added, *"Every single moment in life is a gift from God."* His son, in a live interview, said, "My father has everything; he didn't need to do any of this—to play golf, go on a yacht, retire with a great life he accomplished—but he's doing it solely because he loves this country."

Remarkably, he was struck in the right ear, which my son-in-law pointed out symbolically mirrors the Jewish tradition of piercing the ear of a slave who chooses to remain with his master instead of going free, as described in the Torah. This act signifies a failure to heed God's commandment to serve only Him, and instead, choosing to serve a human master. In Kiddushin 22B it writes: "A person gets his ear pierced because he did not learn the lesson that he is meant to be a servant of God and nobody else." This profound symbolism touched me deeply, especially considering President Trump's acknowledgment of God's protection. His experience and subsequent statements reflected a new-found humility and dedication to serving a higher purpose, akin to the lesson imparted in the Gemara.

During his first speech after the attempted assassination, President Trump spoke about his mission to rectify America, emphasizing his commitment to returning the country to its foundational values. He expressed his love for the Jewish people and his desire to secure peace and stability. *"To the entire world, we want our hostages back and they better be back when I assume office because you will be paying a very big price."* (he acts like a big brother to us). He got a standing ovation. He did not need to say this at all, having to worry about himself and the American people, but he didn't care. He loves the Jewish people immensely. His speech resonated with many, showcasing a leader who had undergone a significant spiritual and emotional transformation.

I actually took the liberty of writing to Donald Trump a couple of weeks ago in which I would like to share excerpts.

To President Donald Trump,

Enclosed is one of my most recent articles titled "The Verdict on President Donald Trump." In this article, I discuss what our great Jewish Sages of blessed memory wrote over 1500 years ago in the Talmud and how it relates to current events regarding you. I hope this will inspire you to carry on your great work of eradicating evil in America and the world, paving the way for the Jewish people to return home, welcome the Messiah, and rebuild the Third Temple.

In the article, I explained how the verdict against you was based on total falsehoods, according to my understanding and interpretation of our Rabbis of old. The article was published in the Jewish Tribune newspaper in England and posted in the Lakewoodscoop in late June and then on Monday,

July 1, the Supreme Court rejected the claims, aligning with my argument that the allegations were unfounded.

I also want to express my gratitude for your significant actions: moving the embassy to Jerusalem, giving the Golan Heights back to the Jewish people, and making peace between Israel and the Arab nations. Your efforts in these areas have been monumental and deeply appreciated.

May God bless you and give you strength, together with the First Lady, to continue the vital task you have been given by God: to eradicate the evil permitted by the Democrats, such as abortion, same-sex marriages, and other actions against the word of God. May true justice be served upon them and may they be removed from their positions as soon as possible, cleansing America and the world. I hope this inspires you to continue your noble work.

Yours sincerely,
Rabbi Dovid Abenson
Lakewood, New Jersey

In this letter, I blessed President Trump, encouraging him to continue his vital work and expressing my hope that he would recognise the divine intervention in his life. In last week's Torah portion, Parshas Balak, contains a fascinating lesson. Balaam, who intended to curse the Jewish people, ended up blessing them instead. The verse (24:9) states, כרע שכב כארי וכלביא מי יקימנו מברכיך ברוך וארריך ארור and Onkelos translates it as follows

נוח ישרי בתקוף כאריא וכליתא לית מלכות דתזעזעיניה בריכך יהון בריכין וליטיך יהון ליטין He crouches and lies [rests and dwells with might] like a lion, and, being a lion, who would dare rouse him? [No kingdom can cause him fear.] **Those who bless you are blessed, and those who curse you are cursed.**

The power of blessings and curses is profound. When Jewish people bless someone, even a non-Jew, the blessings take effect. On July 8, I blessed President Trump, wishing for peace and the fulfillment of his mission to support the Jewish people and secure peace. Subsequently, I prayed for the removal of those who promote actions against God's will, such as the current administration's support for policies contrary to traditional values. Then the next day I heard that even within Joe Biden's own party, there are those who wish to remove him from office to rid America of the perceived evil he has perpetuated. such as the open borders policy, which has led to increased drug trafficking and crime. They see President Biden and his administration as the source of the nation's troubles and desire a change in leadership to restore order and safety.

I've been humbled by my letter. A gesture of blessings and curses has been fulfilled, the recognition of Hashem which I never dreamed of. It's a truly humble experience for me in the service of Hashem. I had just finished writing this article on the morning of Sunday, July 21st and later that afternoon President Biden resigned and stepped down, not seeking reelection for a second term. I am in awe!

This remarkable series of events and the apparent fulfillment of these blessings and curses highlight the power and influence of the Jewish People's tefillos and blessings.

I would like to conclude with a beautiful Midrash Rabbah Shemos from Mishpatim (30:4).

We find that every time the word "Toledos" appears in the Chumash it is written defectively, such as missing a vav, except for: "This is the toledos of the heavens and the earth" (*Bereshis* 2:4), and "this is the toledos of Peretz" (*Ruth* 4:18). And there is a compelling reason why it says: "This is the toledos of the heavens and the earth" in full. It is because Hashem created His world, and there was no angel of death in the world. That is why it is complete. When Adam and Eve sinned, Hashem minimised all the toledos in the Chumash. When Peretz arose, his toledos became full, because Moshiach will emerge from him, in whose days Hashem will eliminate death, as it is stated:בלע המות לנצח "He will eliminate death forever" (*Yeshayahu* 25:8).

May all mankind merit the fulfillment of the prophecy of Yeshayahu "בלע המות לנצח" ("He will eliminate death forever") and also the fulfillment of Yeshayahu Hanavi (*Yeshayahu* 2:4).

וכתתו חרבותם לאתים וחניתותיהם למזמרות לא־ישא גוי אל־גוי חרב ולא־ילמדו עוד מלחמה...

They shall beat their swords into plowshares and their spears into pruning hooks; nation shall not lift the sword against nation, neither shall they learn war anymore.

May this happen b'karov mamash.

THE FIFTH GALUS

As I have mentioned in my previous articles, the prophecies are coming true in our days. Events that the Torah and prophets prophesied about thousands of years ago, discussing the end of times, are unfolding before our eyes. It is essential to delve deeper into these prophecies, as they are increasingly relevant to the current events happening to us daily. One such profound insight comes from Rav Chaim Vital, a student of the Arizal, in his *Etz Daas Tov* commenting on *Tehillim* 124.

We already know from the prophets, particularly Daniel, that there are four exiles: Bavel, Madai, Yavan, and Edom. However, in the future, at the end of the days, there will be another galus (exile) of Yishmael. This fifth galus will be the final one and more challenging than all the four previous ones. Yishmael is called a פרא אדם (Pere Adam). This is the meaning of Dovid Hamelech's words: "If not for Hashem being with us, Adam would come against us." Yishmael was called "Adam" because he had the merit of being a son of Avraham and for having a bris milah, which makes this galus so much harder.

How do you translate פרא אדם?

A remarkable midrash in Esther Rabbah (1:17) presents places and nations that have disproportionate amounts of various characteristics:

תני בשם רבי נתן מעשרה מדות אלו,עשרה חלקים של טפשות בעולם, תשעה
בישמעאלים ואחד בכל העולם

106

It is taught in the name of Rabbi Natan about these ten measures: There are ten portions of foolishness in the world, nine among the Ishmaelites and one in the rest of the world.

The Radal writes in that Yishmael is called a פרא אדם, which translates to "wild donkey of a man." (*Bereishis* 16:12)

What does פרא אדם have to do with foolishness טפשות?

We all know that foolishness implies brainlessness and a lack of intelligence.

Why not call Arabs cockroaches? Cockroaches keep popping up even when killed, much like the recurring threats from Gaza. To wipe them out completely would make more sense. But the term "wild ass" is used instead. Donkeys are known to be highly unintelligent and brainless—that's what foolishness means. Consequences don't seem to affect the Arabs at all.

Did those who committed the atrocities on October 7th think they would get away with killing over 1200 Jews? Are they nuts? No country in the world would accept such a thing. Why do they do it? Because they are like wild asses, completely brainless and foolish. In fact, the Iranian regime knows this and uses proxies around Israel to do their dirty work. These proxies, motivated by money, include groups like Hizballah and others in Yemen and neighboring countries. Do you think Yemen would dare to attack America? They wouldn't, but their foolishness drives them to irrational actions.

This lack of intelligence is evident on university campuses around America and England, and around the world where demonstrations and violence occur under the guise of freedom of speech. The English Prime Minister is taking measures by banning these people and revoking visas. Didn't they consider the consequences of their actions? It's not their country, but they still act foolishly.

The angel said to Hagar, "Your children will be numerous, but they will be wild asses," highlighting their unintelligence.

Hagar did not complain when the angel said her children would be טפשות, brainless fools. What type of blessing is that? However, the verse says something fascinating:

הוא יהיה ידו בכל ויד כל בו ועל־פני כל־אחיו ישכן

His hand will be upon all, and everyone's hand upon him, and before all his brothers he will dwell.

Onkelos explains:

והוא יהא מרוד באנשא הוא יהא צריך לכלא וידא דבני אנשא יהון צריכין ליה ועל אפי כל אחוהי ישרי

He will be a wild, uncivilised man [rebel against people]. His hand [will be] against everyone [He will need everyone] and everyone's hand will be against him [and everyone's hand will need him]; and in the presence of all his brothers he will dwell.

One of my rebbeim interpreted this as referring to the Arabs having oil. This could be why President Biden stopped oil production in America, to fulfill this prophecy and blessing for Hagar. They would not worry about financials; they have so much money, and we see today that the success of the Arabs is only through the oil they have. And that is a blessing, but nevertheless, the concept of foolishness remains. No parent wants their kids to be considered foolish or brainless, as it implies a lack of foresight and understanding of the consequences of their actions. So what type of blessing is it to be called a wild ass?

Ramban answers this dilemma (see *Ramban Bereishis* 16:6) :

תענה שרי ותברח מפניה חטאה אמנו בעניי הזה וגם אברהם בהניחו לעשות כן וישמע ה' אל עניה ונתן לה בן שיהא פרא אדם לענות זרע אברהם ושרה בכל מיני העינוי

*Sarai dealt harshly with her, and she fled from before her face. Our mother did transgress by this affliction, and Abraham also by permitting her to do so. And so, G-d heard her [Hagar's] affliction and gave her a son who would be a wild-ass of a man, to afflict the seed of Abraham and Sarah **with all kinds of affliction**.*

In order to afflict all types of afflictions, one has to be טפשות, refusing to submit to the norms of society—a coarse mentality. That is

108

the characteristic of פרא אדם, a wild ass of a man who does not accept societal norms. Although it sounds strange, the Arabs being טפשות is not a negative; rather, it is a positive trait that allows them to afflict the Jewish people. חטאה אמנו בעוני הזה Our mother did transgress by this affliction.

Rav Chaim Vital writes that Yishmael's name is ישמעקל because in the future Klal Yisroel will cry out immensely at the end of days to Hashem due to the affliction caused by the Arabs, and then ישמעם קל, Hashem will hear them and bring the Final Redemption.

Understanding these prophecies and their implications can provide us with insight and perhaps even a strategy to address the ongoing challenges posed by this fifth galus. While the foolishness of the פרא אדם presents significant challenges, it also reaffirms the ultimate promise of redemption and the enduring strength of the Jewish people.

PART THREE
A SIGNED LETTER FROM PRESIDENT DONALD J. TRUMP: PRAISING AND BLESSING RABBI DOVID ABENSON FOR THE TREMENDOUS WORK HE DOES FOR THE JEWISH PEOPLE

DONALD J. TRUMP

August 19, 2024

Rabbi Dovid Abenson
Lakewood, New Jersey

Dear Rabbi Abenson,

Thank you for your very thoughtful letter.

The outpouring of support and well wishes from compassionate Americans like you means a great deal to me and my family.

Melania and I are inspired by your leadership and enduring faithfulness. Your spirit of excellence and dedication to your congregation means so much to your community and our county.

Please know that I remain forever steadfast in my resolve to fight for the America we cherish!

May God continue to bless you and your family.

Sincerely,

112

"A Signed Letter from President Donald J. Trump: Praising and Blessing Rabbi Dovid Abenson for the Tremendous Work He Does for the Jewish People"

I am humbled to share with the Jewish community a letter I recently received from the President of the United States, Donald J. Trump. In his letter, he expressed admiration for my efforts in "saving Jewish souls" and strengthening our community, offering a heartfelt blessing: "May God continue to bless you and your family."

Receiving such recognition from a non-Jewish leader who demonstrates genuine and unwavering love and support for the Jewish people and acknowledges the existence of Hashem is truly inspiring. President Trump's commitment to klal Yisroel, both in America and Israel, is exceptional. No other president since the founding of the United States has shown such deep regard for the Jewish people. Despite his demanding schedule filled with campaigning and rallies, Mr. Trump took the time to write this letter, with a handwritten signature, reflecting his deep understanding and commitment to my work.

This letter, which highlights his steadfast support for klal Yisroel, should inspire all Jews—both religious and secular—who have traditionally voted for Democrats, to reconsider and vote for Trump on the 5th of November. The American people need his leadership, and the world needs him back in the White House to address the challenges that the Democrats and the Biden Administration have unleashed.

Unfortunately, the Biden Administration's agenda is deliberately defying Hashem's will. We are witnessing same-sex marriages, allowing the killing of unborn babies, a disregard for the law of the land, and opening borders to murderers and drug dealers which is leading to thousands of deaths from drugs and violence. This blatant disregard for morality and safety is a direct affront to the values we hold dear.

Chazal teaches in Sanhedrin 56a that the descendants of Noach, (which is technically the whole of humanity), were commanded to observe the Seven Noachide Laws, establish courts of judgment; prohibit cursing Hashem's name; prohibit avodah zara; forbidding forbidden sexual relations; prohibit bloodshed; prohibit robbery, and eating a limb from a living animal. Disregarding these moral principles is a violation of our values, as President Reagan emphasised in 1982, highlighting the necessity of upholding these ethical standards. I mentioned this in my letter to President Trump.

May this new year bring about the eradication of all who support and promote policies that threaten our values and future. The Rambam states in *Hilchos Melachim* (9:14) that a non-Jew who transgresses any of the Seven Noachide Laws is liable to the death penalty; this includes those, like the Democrat Party and other groups, who endorse such destructive actions. Let truth and justice prevail, guiding us on a path of strength and moral clarity.

May we all witness the fulfillment of what we daven for each morning in *Aleinu*: *'And all mankind will invoke Your Name, to turn back to You, all the wicked of the earth. They will realise and know, all the inhabitants of the world, that to You, every knee must bend, every tongue must swear [allegiance to You]. Before You Hashem our God, they will bow and prostrate themselves, and to the glory of Your Name give honor. And they will all accept [upon themselves] the yoke of Your kingdom, and You will reign over them, soon, forever and ever. For the kingdom is Yours, and to all eternity, You will reign in glory….*

Wishing you all a kesiva v'chasima tova!

Rabbi Dovid Abenson

8 July 2024

To President Donald J. Trump,

*Enclosed is one of my most recent articles titled "**The Verdict on President Donald Trump.**" In this article, I discuss what our great Jewish Sages of blessed memory wrote over 1500 years ago in the Talmud and how it relates to current events regarding you. I hope this will inspire you to carry on your great work of eradicating evil in America and the world, paving the way for the Jewish people to return home, welcome the Messiah, and rebuild the Third Temple.*

In the article, I explained how the verdict against you was based on total falsehoods, according to my understanding and interpretation of our Rabbis of old. The article was published in the Jewish Tribune in England on Wednesday, June 26th, and in the Lakewood Scoop on Thursday, June 20th. Then, on Monday, July 1, the Supreme Court rejected the claims, aligning with my argument that the allegations were unfounded.

I also want to express my gratitude for your significant actions: moving the embassy to Jerusalem, giving the Golan Heights back to the Jewish people, and making peace between Israel and the Arab nations. Your efforts in these areas have been monumental and deeply appreciated.

May God bless you and give you strength, together with the First Lady, to continue the vital task you have been given by God: to eradicate the evil permitted by the Democrats, such as abortion, same-sex marriages, and other actions against the word of God. May true justice be served upon them

115

and may they be removed from their positions as soon as possible, cleansing America and the world. I hope this inspires you to continue your noble work.

Yours sincerely,

Rabbi Dovid Abenson

August 7, 2024

To President Donald J. Trump,

I hope this letter finds you and the First Lady in good health. Enclosed is an article titled" An Open Miracle by Hashem for the World To See" which I recently posted in The Lakewood Scoop and published in the Jewish Tribune in England. I am sending this to provide both of you with strength and encouragement, especially in light of the recent assassination attempt on your life.

Your mission to confront and eradicate the moral decay that has taken hold in America is more critical now than ever. The forces of evil, led by certain political entities—most notably the Democrat Party—are actively working to dismantle the very fabric of our society. Their actions, which openly defy divine principles, endorse immorality, and normalise practices that are in direct opposition to God's teachings, are a severe threat to the values that have long upheld a just and righteous society. It is clear that the Democrat Party and all those who support them harbor a deep disdain for God and the moral order He established, choosing instead to promote a godless agenda that seeks to erase the divine from the public sphere. This party, the Democrats, and all those who associate with them must be eradicated once and for all, and you, President Trump, were given that mission by God to do so.

The Seven Noahide Laws, which form the moral bedrock of humanity, are clear in their directives. They highlight the necessity of justice, the sanctity of life, and the importance of creating a world that reflects God's will. Yet, these sacred laws—prohibiting idolatry, blasphemy, murder, theft, sexual immorality, cruelty to animals, and unjust legal systems—are being flagrantly disregarded by those who have strayed far from the path of righteousness. This erosion of moral standards has led to the widespread acceptance of behaviors that are in direct conflict with the divine commandments that have guided humanity for millennia.

Your unwavering commitment to upholding these universal principles is reminiscent of the courageous leadership demonstrated by President Reagan. In 1982, President Reagan forged a tradition of mutual encouragement with the Lubavitcher Rebbe, Rabbi Menachem Mendel Schneerson, who was a steadfast advocate for moral clarity and the fight against evil. This tradition, marked by Reagan's proclamation Recognising the Rebbe's 80th birthday as "Education Day, USA," served as a beacon of hope and guidance in a troubled world. I trust that you, too, will draw strength from this legacy as you continue your critical work.

You have been entrusted with a sacred mission from God to uphold these timeless values and to stand firm against those who seek to undermine them. I am fully committed to supporting you in this battle. I pray that my articles and word of mouth will mobilize the religious Jewish community to rally behind you and vote in great numbers on Tuesday, November 5, 2024.

May you and the First Lady be blessed with the strength and health to carry out the vital work that has been divinely appointed to you. The future of our nation, and indeed the world, depends on it.

Yours sincerely

Rabbi Dovid Abenson

4 Sept 2024

To President Donald J. Trump,

I am profoundly humbled to have received your heartfelt letter. Your words of admiration for my efforts in "saving Jewish souls" and strengthening our community are deeply appreciated. Your blessing, "May God continue to bless you and your family," was very moving.

It is truly inspiring to receive such recognition from a true leader who demonstrates genuine and unwavering love and support for the Jewish people, whilst also acknowledging the existence of God. Your commitment to the Jewish people, both in America and Israel, is exceptional. No president in the history of the United States has shown such profound regard for the Jewish people as you have. Despite your demanding schedule filled with campaigning and rallies, you took the time to write this letter, with a handwritten signature, reflecting your deep understanding and commitment to my work.

Your steadfast support for Jewish people should serve as an inspiration to all Jews—both religious and secular—who have traditionally voted for Democrats, to reconsider and support you in the upcoming election. The American people need your leadership, and the world needs you back in the White House to address the challenges that the current administration has unleashed.

Unfortunately, the agenda of the current administration is in direct defiance of God's will. We are witnessing the endorsement of same-sex marriages, the tragic allowance of killing unborn babies, a disregard for the law of the land, and open borders that permit murderers and drug dealers to enter, leading to countless deaths from drugs and violence. This blatant disregard for morality and safety is an affront to the values we hold dear.

Our Rabbis teach that all of humanity, as descendants of Noah, is commanded to observe the Seven Noahide Laws: establishing courts of justice, prohibiting cursing God's name, prohibiting idol worship, forbidding forbidden sexual relations, prohibiting bloodshed, prohibiting robbery, and abstaining from eating a limb from a living animal. Disregarding these moral principles is a violation of society, as President Reagan emphasised in 1982, underscoring the necessity of upholding these ethical standards. I mentioned this in my previous letter to you, Mr. President, and I remain steadfast in my belief that these values must be upheld.

118

In Bereshis (12:3), God promises to Abraham, "I will bless those who bless you, and whoever curses you I will curse." By blessing the Jewish people through your unwavering support, you align yourself with this Divine promise. I am confident that you will be blessed in this world and the next, including being granted the strength and wisdom to turn America around for the good when you return to the presidency.

It would be my great honor to bestow upon you a special blessing, which is a revered tradition when you become president:

בָּרוּךְ אַתָּה ה' אלקינו מלך העולם, שנתן מכבודו לבשר ודם

Blessed are You our God, King of the universe, who has given His glory to mortals.

As we approach the Jewish new year, my prayer is for the swift obliteration of all those who support and promote policies that threaten our values and our future. The well-revered Rabbi of old, Mamonides, states in Hilchos Melachim (9:14) that a non-Jew who transgresses any of the Seven Noahide Laws is liable to the death penalty; this includes those, like the current administration of the Democrats and other groups, who endorse such destructive actions. Let truth and justice prevail, guiding us on a path of strength and moral clarity.

Sincerely,

Rabbi Dovid Abenson

Sept. 11

Dear President Donald J. Trump,

I hope this letter finds you and the First Lady in good health. I write to you today with a deep sense of urgency and a heavy heart following the tragic events in Israel. The brutal murder of six hostages by Hamas and the killing of three police officers in the West Bank have shocked and horrified us all. I want to express my profound gratitude for your swift and unequivocal condemnation of these heinous acts of terror. Your unwavering support and genuine love for the Jewish people are unparalleled, and your leadership has stood out on the world stage like no other.

It is deeply disturbing that, during this critical time, the British government has chosen to withhold arms support to Israel. This decision sets a dangerous precedent—a tacit approval of Hamas's atrocities. As I have previously mentioned, the words of God to Abraham are as true now as they were in biblical times: "I will bless those who bless you, and he who curses you, I will curse" (Bereshis 12:3). History has repeatedly shown that nations rise and fall based on their treatment of the Jewish people.

Mr. President, your leadership has always been a beacon of strength and resolve. Under your administration, the Jewish people knew they had a true friend who would stand with them, defend their God-given right to the land of Israel, and hold terrorists accountable. Your support for Israel sent a clear message to the world that evil would not be tolerated, and your actions commanded both respect and fear.

However, as we witness the horrors of today, we must acknowledge that the crisis Israel faces is not merely political or military. I have enclosed my recent article discussing the spiritual conflict between the Jews and Arabs, known as the "Fifth Exile," which the Jewish people are enduring before the coming of the Messiah.

The well-being of the Jewish people is tied to our adherence to God's commandments. As the Torah teaches us in Deuteronomy (28:15): "But it shall come to pass, if you do not listen to the voice of the Lord your God… all these curses shall come upon you." When we stray, calamities follow, just as foretold in the Torah. The Jewish people have repeatedly suffered from wars, terror attacks, expulsions, and other forms of persecution, for millennia since biblical times to the present day.

Mr. President, you have the unique ability to influence global leaders, particularly Prime Minister Netanyahu, a man who has always admired your strength and commitment. I respectfully urge you to encourage him to take bold and decisive steps toward a renewed commitment to Torah and its commandments in Israel. This effort should begin with Netanyahu himself, along with all members of the Knesset. The leadership must set the example by observing Shabbos and adhering to the commandments, thereby drawing secular Israelis back to their faith and heritage.

In addition, the Israeli Supreme Court's legal system, deeply entrenched in secular laws from the Ottoman and British eras, needs a profound transformation to reflect the Jewish essence of the state. Israel must be governed by Torah law to ensure both spiritual and material prosperity. Just as you have faced false accusations from the DOJ and witnessed the corrupt actions of Democrat judges and politicians trying to undermine your leadership, Israel faces a similar crisis of corruption in its judiciary and political systems. Your commitment to "draining the swamp" in America resonates deeply with us, and this urgent need for cleansing extends to Israel as well. The Jewish people are yearning for a return to the purity of the Torah, which should guide every aspect of our lives. Your leadership could be instrumental in this monumental task, helping us restore the divine guidance that was given to Moses at Mount Sinai and bringing the Jewish people back to their sacred heritage.

This corruption extends further to the issue of the so-called Palestinian state. It is a lie with no historical or biblical basis. The concept of a "Palestinian state" was fabricated by Yasser Arafat and perpetuated by those who seek to undermine Israel's legitimate claim to the land. Nowhere in the Bible is there mention of a Palestinian state given to the Arabs.

Rashi, the foremost Jewish commentator, explains in his commentary on Bereshis (1:1) why the Torah begins with the creation of the world. He writes that if the nations of the world accuse the Jewish people of being thieves for taking the land of Canaan, the response is that the entire earth belongs to God. He created it and gave it to whomever He saw fit, and it was His will to give the land of Israel to the Jewish people.

The land of Israel, including Gaza, was given by God exclusively to the Jewish people, as promised to Abraham, Isaac, and Jacob. This divine covenant is clearly stated in the Torah, with specific references to the territory that includes Gaza. In Bereshis (15:18-21), God made a solemn promise to Abraham: "To your descendants, I give this land, from the river of Egypt to the great river, the Euphrates."

This vast territory includes Gaza, part of the ancient land of Canaan, which was given to the Jewish people as an everlasting inheritance. Furthermore, in Bereshis (17:8), God reiterates the promise: "I will give to you and to your descendants after you the land in which you are a stranger, all the land of Canaan, for an everlasting possession." This promise is eternal, and there is no room for compromise or division of the land, as it belongs solely to the Jewish people by divine decree.

The Messianic Era and Your Role of Leadership

As Isaiah prophesied, "And they shall beat their swords into plowshares… neither shall they learn war anymore" (Isaiah 2:4). This vision of peace will only become a reality when the Jewish people fully return to the path of the Torah. You, Mr. President, are uniquely positioned to help guide us toward that future. Just as you showed unwavering resolve during your time in office, declaring "Fight, fight, fight!" Even in the face of an assassination attempt, we now need that same strength to inspire a spiritual awakening for the Jewish people.

With your influence, you can inspire the Jewish people to return to their Father in Heaven and fulfill their divine mission. Through spiritual renewal and adherence to God's commandments, the Jewish people can lead the world toward true peace. As it says in the Torah, "The Lord will fight for you; you need only to be quiet" (Exodus 14:14). Our battles, both physical and spiritual, must be fought with faith in God, not with a single bullet.

Thank you for your unwavering support, your courage, and your love for the Jewish people. May we soon witness peace and the fulfillment of the prophecies in Isaiah (2:4) and Micah (4:3), when the nations will no longer lift up swords, and true peace will reign in the land, with the coming of Mashiach (Messiah) speedily in our days, Amen.

With deepest respect and gratitude,

Rabbi Dovid Abenson

27 Sept 2024

Dear President Donald J. Trump,

I hope this letter finds you and the First Lady in good health.

Enclosed is my latest article, along with the accompanying letter, which I have sent to over 1,100 Jewish friends and associates, rallying them behind your mission and encouraging them to forward this message to their Jewish and non-Jewish contacts, urging them to vote for you on the 5th of November. With God's help, I believe this will create a ripple effect, inspiring them to share it with their wider networks. My goal is to reach millions of people nationwide, encouraging them to vote for you.

If necessary, I can also send this directly to your sons and your son-in-law, Jared Kushner, both in letter and email form, to ensure it reaches their associates and supporters.

We must unite now. I firmly believe that you have been chosen by God to lead this critical fight. The world has already witnessed multiple assassination attempts against you, and once again, God has saved you. Now, Iran seeks to do the same. As you mentioned in one of your public addresses, the FBI should have unlocked the cell phones of those plotting against you, as they have done in the past, but it seems they have refused to act. It is ironic that they do not wish to uncover the connections inspiring these assassins. All of this points to one clear fact: you have been chosen to stand against this evil. You have emerged unscathed, showing the true strength of a leader.

You lead not out of fear, but out of love for this country. Like King David, who fought on the front lines for his people, you stand at the forefront, leading this battle, risking your life for America. You do not simply delegate; you act. This is the mark of a true leader—one who does not sit back but faces danger head-on with courage and resolve. May God continually protect you and give you the strength to carry on and lead America to victory.

You are the only one with the strength and vision to save America from the evil forces that the Democrats have brazenly unleashed upon this nation. They defiantly oppose God's will and threaten our core values. With God's guidance and your leadership, we will drive out this darkness and secure victory for the American people.

This is a battle between good and evil, and you are the one destined to lead us to victory. I am ready to do everything in my power to support you in this divine mission.

May God bless you and the First Lady, guiding you both in this crucial endeavor.

Yours sincerely,

Rabbi Dovid Abenson

Other Books By Rabbi Dovid Abenson

The Following books are available

A Groundbreaking Addition to the Jewish Market

RABBI MATTISYAHU'S LEGACY CONTINUES.

By scanning the barcodes inside, experience Rebbe's teachings in a whole new way. Hear his voice, see his wisdom, and be uplifted by the inspiration that has impacted so many.

Essential for Mechanchim and Parents–bring the Rebbe's guidance into your home or classroom.

Purchase today at http://atalmidsjourney.com/

A Practical Guide to Success in Independant Torah Learning

Testimonials

"Your book's pile at the bookstore was the lowest so I assumed it must be a good seller and promptly bought it.... I couldn't believe it. *I was glued to it.* I couldn't put the book down...*I wanted to call you right away but it took me a few days to pluck up the courage"*
— Rabbi M, 43-year-old shoel umeshiv with over a decade of experience

"Rabbi Abenson, I'm so happy that you had the guts to write such an important, well-written book on education....*Everyone should have this book"*
— Rabbi T, rebbi for 18 years

"Would you be able to help my 8-year-old son Yaakov? He is fully medicated. Can you help me, too? I'm 38 years old and FFB. I've been through the Yeshiva system. I'm unable to learn on my own. *Your book caught my attention in the Jewish bookstore. It spoke to me.* I use ArtScroll; it's all in English"
— Elchonon, 38-year-old balabos

"No one in all my yeshivos had noticed my weaknesses. *I thought I just didn't have a brain for learning"*
— Shaya, 24-year-old bochur (now back on track after finding my book in Geula.)

FIRST STEPS IN KIRUV

https://www.amazon.com/First-Steps-Kiruv-Rabbi-Abenson/dp/1568712537
https://menuchapublishers.com/products/first-steps-in-kiruv
https://breslev.com/product/first-steps-in-kiruv/

"From the Desk of Rabbi Dovid Abenson"

This is not just another book; it is the culmination of over four decades of teaching, wisdom, and profound Torah insights. Divided into two parts, the first section presents a collection of articles I've meticulously crafted for leading publications. These writings delve into essential topics such as the "Ask the Rabbi" series, Jewish education, anti-missionary strategies and kiruv techniques all viewed through the timeless lens of the Torah.

This book is an invaluable resource for parents and educators committed to deepening their understanding and skillfully navigating the challenges of today's world. Each page is designed to spark thoughtful reflection, inspire meaningful action, and provide the clarity needed to thrive in a constantly changing environment.

The second part is a crash course in Lashon HaKodesh, based on the methods I use in my teaching, along with a comprehensive overview of the training courses I offer. This section is perfect for those looking to enhance their knowledge, advance their teaching careers, and effectively educate their talmidim.

Don't miss this opportunity to gain access to these transformative insights. Secure your copy now and embark on a journey that will enrich your life, your family, and your community. This book is more than just a resource—it's a guide, a tool, and a source of inspiration that remains both timeless and relevant in the study of the Torah.

Order your copy today and take the next step in your educational journey!

Order now at: rabbidovidabenson.com